CRAP TEAMS

CRAP TEAMS

GEOFF TIBBALLS

Michael O'Mara Books Limited

First published in 2005 by
... Books Limited
... Lion Yard
... Road
... W4 7NQ

Copyright © Michael O'Mara ...

A CIP catalogue record for this book is available from the British Library.

ISBN (10-digit): 1-84317-111-2

ISBN (13-digit): 978-1-84317-111-9

3 5 7 9 10 8 6 4 2

Designed and typeset by www.envydesign.co.uk

Printed and bound in Italy by L.E.G.O.

www.mombooks.com

CONTENTS

Crystal Palace: 1980-81	42
Chelsea: 1982-83	45
Derby County: 1983-84	48
Wolverhampton Wanderers: 1984-85	51
Birmingham City: 1985-86	54
Glasgow Rangers: 1985-86	57
Manchester United: 1986-87	60
Sunderland: 1986-87	63
Tottenham Hotspur: 1987-88	66
Portsmouth: 1987-88	69
Newcastle United: 1988-89	72
Charlton Athletic: 1989-90	75
West Ham United: 1991-92	78
England: 1992 European Championships Finals	81
Birmingham City: 1993-94	84
Arsenal: 1994-95	87
Ipswich Town: 1994-95	90
Southampton: 1995-96	94
Bolton Wanderers: 1995-96	97

There is a lot to be said for supporting one of the smaller clubs. It's rather like driving a Minardi or being a Dutch skier – expectation is usually lower than a chavette's IQ. As a result defeat is easy to take. Weekends aren't ruined, relationships aren't wrecked and the cat doesn't cower behind the sofa just because your striker is about as good in the air as Dennis Bergkamp. But if you follow one of the Premiership big boys, it's a different story. At Chelsea a crisis is two successive draws; at Rotherham a crisis is when they run out of meat pies. So, in a sport where money talks louder than a Gary Megson touchline blast and where even agents have agents, it is always refreshing to see the Premiership fat cats fail to get the cream.

As a humble Millwall supporter of forty years' standing (and more recently sitting), it has therefore been a joy to recall those seasons when the top clubs struggled miserably – when the trophy polisher at Old Trafford was made redundant due to lack of work, when the Gunners fired blanks and when there was more excitement at the Chelsea Flower Show than at Stamford Bridge. And on the international front, there is Scotland's greatest shame since *The White Heather Club*, and the summer when the only thing the Germans won was the race for the sunbeds. So I would like to thank Kate Gribble and the team at Michael O'Mara Books, as well as all of those overpaid footballers and underachieving managers, for making this book possible.

Geoff Tibballs, 2005

SHEFFIELD WEDNESDAY

1969-70

- ⊕ **League: 22nd (Division 1)**
- ⊕ **FA Cup: 1-2 Scunthorpe United, round 4**
- ⊕ **League Cup: 0-1 Bournemouth, round 2 replay**

It was a time when girls' legs were buried beneath maxi skirts (the only fashion item to require more material than a pair of curtains) and Rolf Harris topped the charts with 'Two Little Boys'. No wonder people were so sorry to see the back of the sixties. It was also the year that Neil Armstrong took Man's first steps on the moon, maybe unaware that in a corner of Yorkshire Danny Williams faced an even greater challenge –

A FORTHRIGHT BLUNTNESS THAT WOULD MAKE JOSÉ MOURINHO SEEM SHY AND RETIRING

that of keeping Sheffield Wednesday in the First Division. An ex-Yorkshire miner not to be confused with the guy who sang 'Moon River', Danny Williams joined Wednesday in the summer of '69, an appointment so popular that many years later Bryan Adams felt compelled to write a song about it. Bryan reckoned 'those were the best days of my life' but also noted 'I guess nothin' can last forever', which is generally thought to refer to the Owls' defeat by Scunthorpe in the fourth round of the Cup.

While the young Mr Adams was getting his first checked shirt, Williams had been making a name for himself at Swindon,

Wednesday's Alan Warboys, an old-fashioned battering ram of a centre-forward.

leading the little Wiltshire club to promotion from the Third Division and to a memorable League Cup triumph. So his arrival at Hillsborough was largely welcomed. However the team, which had narrowly avoided relegation in 1968, was in decline. Williams, with a forthright bluntness that would make José Mourinho seem shy and retiring, declared publicly that he had only three decent players – David Ford, Peter Eustace and Wilf Smith – before inexplicably selling all three, although Smith did last until the end of the season. Eustace departed to West Ham for £90,000 in December 1969 and in the same month Ford went to Newcastle in the deal that brought Jackie Sinclair to Hillsborough. By then Wednesday were deep in trouble, going three months between

⚽ ODDBALL

AT THE AGE OF SIXTEEN, THE FUTURE SHEFFIELD WEDNESDAY AND ENGLAND MAN CHRIS WADDLE LANDED A JOB WITH CHEVIOT SEASONING LTD, SUNDERLAND, MAKING SEASONING TO FLAVOUR SAUSAGES AND PIES. HE WENT FOR THE INTERVIEW ON THE BACK OF HIS BROTHER'S MOTORBIKE – BUT COULDN'T GET HIS CRASH HELMET OFF AND HAD TO SIT WEARING IT THROUGHOUT THE INTERVIEW.

September and Boxing Day without a win and crashing out of the League Cup to Third Division Bournemouth. And with finances tighter than a Yorkshireman's grip on his wallet, the outlook was bleak.

The return of lively striker Jack Whitham after injury offered a degree of hope, particularly when he was paired with Alan Warboys, an old-fashioned battering ram of a centre-forward. Warboys possessed the qualities of an albatross: exquisite in the air but clumsy and awkward on the ground. He unsettled defenders with his robust approach but was ultimately unable to contribute enough goals to keep Wednesday up. Five of the last six games ended in defeat, a 2-1 home loss to Manchester City in the final fixture condemning Wednesday to the dreaded drop. Like Warboys, Tommy Craig, a cultured Scottish midfielder with a left foot that could thread a needle, would enjoy better fortune in the lower division. But Williams was not there to see it beyond New Year's Day, and it would be another fourteen years before Wednesday returned to the top flight. They arrived back in the big time to find that Rolf Harris was still singing 'Two Little Boys'.

LIVERPOOL
1969-70

- ⚽ **League: 5th (Division 1)**
- ⚽ **FA Cup: 0-1 Watford, round 6**
- ⚽ **League Cup: 2-3 Manchester City, round 3**
- ⚽ **Fairs Cup: 3-3 (aggregate, lost on away goals) Vitoria Setubal, round 2**

Like a man unwilling to throw out a favourite suit, Liverpool manager Bill Shankly couldn't bear to admit that many of the players who had served him so well in the past were now ready for football's equivalent of a car boot sale. But by 1969 Liverpool were an ageing team whose value was more likely to be determined on the *Antiques Roadshow* than by a transfer

THE ANFIELD DAD'S ARMY WERE PRESSED INTO SERVICE

tribunal. True, Shankly had attempted to plan for the future by making Wolves striker Alun Evans football's first £100,000 teenager, but Evans would spend almost as much time in the treatment room as the penalty box. So the Anfield Dad's Army were pressed into active service once more.

The season began well enough and Liverpool sat on top of the table in mid-September. To outsiders their subsequent decline must have been as incomprehensible as Hamlet's soliloquy read by Lester Piggott, but an early exit from Europe was a warning of things to come. Then in the same week that the team lost 4-1 at home to Manchester United Roger Hunt, hero of the Kop, left for Bolton. The unspectacular Hunt may have thought charisma fell on December 25 and he was not everyone's ideal striker but, as Shankly used to say, at least he was usually in the right place to miss the chances. Nevertheless it took a Cup defeat to struggling First Division Watford to make the manager finally realize that the only imminent hope of a trophy lay with the local pub quiz.

Indicative of the side's failings in attack was that fullback Chris Lawler was second highest scorer with ten goals. So, belatedly, Shankly began to get rid of the old guard. First out of the door were his fellow Scots – forward Ian St John, centre-half Ron Yeats and 14-stone goalkeeper Tommy Lawrence, affectionately known as 'The Flying Pig'. Built like a generously proportioned space hopper, Lawrence was a popular figure and

⚽ ODDBALL

LIVERPOOL GOALKEEPER DAVID JAMES BLAMED HIS LOSS OF FORM IN 1998 ON SPENDING TOO MANY HOURS AT HOME PLAYING COMPUTER GAMES.

many at the club hoped he would return to Anfield one day as team coach, but only if the usual transport broke down.

The Liverpool team photo from 1969. It was the only time they smiled all season.

WEST HAM UNITED
1970-71

⚽ **League: 20th (Division 1)**
⚽ **FA Cup: 0-4 Blackpool, round 3**
⚽ **League Cup: 1-3 Coventry City, round 3**

Like strawberries and cream, Romeo and Juliet, and Chas and Dave, Jimmy Greaves and West Ham were somehow made for each other. Not because the club was a fitting setting for Greaves to spend the twilight of his glorious career, but because at the time it boasted a drinking culture that was the envy of the Football League. That Bobby Moore always looked such a cool customer was partly due to the fact that he usually had ice in his shorts, along with a slice of lemon. And striker Brian Dear always looked as if he could hold more beer than the average pub cellar. So when Greaves, who on his own admission was drinking heavily by then, landed at Upton Park, he found himself among kindred spirits. Things came to a head when the Hammers were drawn at Blackpool in the third round of the FA Cup. Believing that the match would be postponed because of a frozen pitch, Greaves, Moore, Dear and Clyde Best stayed out late at a Blackpool nightclub on the eve of the tie. But to their horror the game went ahead and the hungover Hammers crashed out of

THEIR DRINKS HAD BEEN LACED MORE EFFECTIVELY THAN THEIR BOOTS

West Ham's Greavsie tries to loop a header over Coventry City goalkeeper Bill Glazier. Not for the first time he was aiming for the bar.

the competition 4-0, in a display that suggested their drinks had been laced more effectively than their boots. When a disgruntled West Ham fan phoned the club and a national newspaper to report the revelling (although to Best's credit, he drank only Coke), manager Ron Greenwood reacted by fining the quartet and dropping Moore and Greaves. For Moore to be stripped of the captaincy was even more humiliating than those TV adverts where he casually dropped into his local.

The Golden Boy was reinstated two games later but the episode was symptomatic of West Ham's troubled season. They had been forced to wait until the eleventh game for their first League win (a Geoff Hurst hat-trick seeing off Burnley) and had fluttered precariously above the relegation zone like a pigeon with damaged tail feathers, a broken wing and another

⚽ ODDBALL

IN 2003 WEST HAM FAN STEVE ADAMS SAT ON ALL 35,056 SEATS AT UPTON PARK TO RAISE MONEY FOR CHARITY. THE MARATHON SIT-IN TOOK HIM NEARLY FIFTY HOURS TO COMPLETE.

pigeon hanging from its legs. But a brief upturn in form in early April enabled them to reach the safety of twentieth place, grateful that the 'three down' rule didn't come into operation for another three years. At the end of the season Greavsie retired to devote more time to his drinking. And Bobby Moore soldiered on. Quite what a young Trevor Brooking, just making his mark in the Hammers' first team, made of it all is open to conjecture. At a guess he probably didn't express an opinion, one way or the other.

WEST BROMWICH ALBION
1972-73

⚽ **League: 22nd (Division 1)**
⚽ **FA Cup: 0-2 Leeds United, round 5**
⚽ **League Cup: 1-2 Liverpool, round 3 replay**

As a loyal lieutenant Don Howe was second to none. But as a manager in his own right he never quite cut the mustard. It was a bit like placing Ernie Wise in sole charge of the act or giving John Prescott the keys to Number Ten. Back in the days when Baggies fan Frank Skinner was still a schoolboy named Chris Collins, and before Bobby Gould's eyebrows were declared a national forest, Howe was boss of an Albion side that had enjoyed twenty-three unbroken years in the top flight. In addition to the much-travelled Gould the manager could call on the services of a number of good honest professionals – people like Tony Brown, Colin Suggett, John Wile, Len Cantello and Asa Hartford – but sadly the talismanic Jeff Astle was missing through injury until February. In his absence it took Albion 305 minutes to register their first goal of the season. Skinner must have sympathized: he and David Baddiel have sometimes waited longer for a laugh.

Frustration began to build at The Hawthorns. Hartford was fined £50 by a civil court after insulting a spectator at Norwich.

IT TOOK ALBION 305 MINUTES TO REGISTER THEIR FIRST GOAL OF THE SEASON

(Under similar guidelines Delia would have been bankrupted following her 2005 rant.) And in February Albion lost 2-1 at West Ham to a goal scored in the ninety-sixth minute after the referee added on no fewer than seven minutes for time wasting. Albion even ran out of gas in the much-missed Texaco Cup, crashing out to Newcastle. In a bid to stop the rot Howe signed fiery winger Willie Johnston from Rangers for a club record £135,000 (even though he was in the middle of an eight-week suspension at the time), plus David Shaw from Oldham. Nicknamed 'the Gazelle' because of his speed, Shaw's poor ball control instead made him as much use as an arthritic elk. At the back, young goalkeeper Peter Latchford was brought in at the expense of veteran bird-watcher John Osborne – but Latchford's inexperience saw him make a series of costly errors. Howe might have been better advised putting Bill Oddie in goal. Any hopes of escape from relegation were shattered by home defeats to fellow strugglers Crystal Palace and Norwich, which left Albion rock bottom at the final reckoning. It would be another three seasons before the club returned to the top division, by which time Don Howe had departed and returned to his role as Best Supporting Actor.

⚽ ODDBALL

WEST BROM'S DUTCH STRIKER FABIAN DE FREITAS HAD A LAME EXCUSE FOR FAILING TO TURN UP FOR THE GAME AGAINST CREWE ON THE AFTERNOON OF EASTER MONDAY 1999 – HE THOUGHT IT WAS AN EVENING KICK-OFF! THE CLUB DESPERATELY TRIED TO PHONE HIM BUT WERE UNABLE TO GET THROUGH TO HIM BECAUSE HIS GIRLFRIEND WAS ON THE LINE. WITHOUT HIM ALBION CRASHED 5-1.

Second to none as a No.2, Don Howe, as No.1 at West Brom, took them into Division 2.

MANCHESTER UNITED
1973-74

⚽ **League: 21st (Division 1)**
⚽ **FA Cup: 0-1 Ipswich Town, round 4**
⚽ **League Cup: 0-1 Middlesbrough, round 2**

Few people came away with anything from a trip to Old Trafford at the start of the seventies … not even their hubcaps. But, as a series of managers tried in vain to show that there was life after the legendary Matt Busby, the team's fortunes began to slide.

By the start of the 1973-74 season the combative Tommy Docherty was in charge of the fine old club. It was like putting the Crown Jewels in the trust of Jade Goody. No respecter of reputations,

BEST WOULD COME AND GO LIKE ACNE

Docherty set about ruffling feathers in his own inimitable style. Bobby Charlton quickly decided to retire and in the summer of 1973 the Doc gave Denis Law a free transfer – a move that enraged United fans. The third member of United's great triumvirate, George Best, was by now hopelessly unreliable. He would come and go like acne. Instead of being United's ace he was the King of Clubs. In October '73 he made one of his many comebacks from the Spanish sunshine, looking hung-over and far from fit. The spirits had clearly been willing but the flesh was weak. Not surprisingly Best's contribution on the pitch that season was minimal, his final appearance for United being against QPR on New Year's Day. As Docherty remarked ruefully: 'He would have been a better player if he had been able to pass a nightclub the way he passed the ball.'

United struggled all season. In March the Manchester derby ended in chaos when, in arguably the greatest mismatch since David and Goliath, United's diminutive Lou Macari squared up to the rugged City defender Mike Doyle. Even Don King might have balked at putting those two in a ring together. Referee Clive 'The Book' Thomas sent the pair off but they refused to go. So Thomas took both teams off the field and, when they eventually returned, it was without Macari and Doyle. This was the ugly face of football … at least until Wayne Rooney came along. The return game was even more memorable: Denis Law, now plying his trade with City, backheeled the

⚽ ODDBALL

SITTING ON THE BENCH BECAUSE OF INJURY, DENIS LAW BECAME SO EXCITED WHEN UNITED SCORED AGAINST REAL MADRID IN THE 1968 EUROPEAN CUP SEMI-FINAL THAT HE PUNCHED THE AIR IN DELIGHT, ONLY TO SMASH HIS FIST THROUGH THE DUGOUT ROOF. HE WAS LEFT WITH A BROKEN BONE IN HIS HAND … AND A LONGER LAY-OFF.

goal that sent United into the Second Division for the first time since 1938. It would prove a real culture shock. For even George Best might have struggled to get a drink on a Tuesday night in Oldham.

Footballing legend George Best. The ball was not the only thing blurred that season; Best's vision the morning after the night before pretty much matched it.

England
1974 WORLD CUP QUALIFIERS

Although Sir Alf Ramsey was marginally less cuddly than a bear with a sore head and PMT, the English public always warmed to him. His bizarre speech patterns – clearly modelled on Parker from *Thunderbirds* – were quintessentially English, while his attitude towards anybody remotely foreign came straight from the days of the Empire. Basically he did for international diplomacy what Faria Alam did to the FA. Obviously winning the World Cup did his reputation no harm but football fans have shorter memories than Ronnie Reagan in his later years and, when premature substitutions cost England dear in Mexico, there were calls for Ramsey's head. Ramsey loved change almost as much as he loved the Scots but by the time of the 1974 World Cup qualifiers, trusted foot soldiers such as Gordon Banks and Bobby Charlton were no longer around, while Bobby Moore's considerable powers were on the wane. England were going through a transitional period, which is a managerial euphemism for 'most of the new players are shite'.

A HARD-EARNED 1-0 WIN IN WALES WAS AN OMINOUS WARNING

England were grouped with Wales and Poland – not the most daunting of obstacles, more junior boys' high jump than Becher's

England's Rodney Marsh trips up as the Welsh start a rendition of 'YMCA'. Frankly, England were more Village People than city slickers in this disastrous campaign.

Brook. But a hard-earned 1-0 win in Wales was an ominous warning. Ramsey disliked flair players but for the return match against Wales he selected Manchester City's Rodney Marsh. Before the game Ramsey told him: 'You don't work hard enough. If you don't work harder tonight, I'll pull you off at half-time.' Marsh replied: 'Christ, we only get a cup of tea and an orange at City!' Ramsey, not noted for his sense of humour, never picked him again. The game ended in a disappointing 1-1 draw but worse was to follow when England travelled to Poland in June 1973. Alan Ball was sent off and Moore had a nightmare. When he woke up, England had been beaten 2-0. So England *had* to defeat Poland at Wembley in October. After a 7-0 demolition of Austria in a warm-up game Ramsey stuck with the same team, led by Martin Peters. According to Ramsey, Peters was ten years ahead of his time, which explains why he was whistling Duran Duran songs as he ran on to the pitch. Of course it all ended in tears. Iron man Norman Hunter made a Dale Winton tackle, Peter Shilton dived like a sack of potatoes and the Poles were a goal up. Allan Clarke equalized but there was no way past the 'clown' in the Polish goal (Brian Clough's description of Jan Tomaszewski). Reluctant to use substitutes after getting a bloody nose in Mexico, Ramsey left it until the eighty-seventh minute before introducing Derby striker Kevin Hector. Even then his instructions were so garbled that the other Kevin on the bench – Keegan – had mistakenly stripped off ready to go on. Ramsey had lost the plot. Six months later he lost his job. Ramsey made no secret of his dislike for most journalists but in

⚽ ODDBALL

AT THE 1962 WORLD CUP FINALS IN CHILE, A DOG RAN ON TO THE PITCH AND URINATED OVER ENGLAND'S JIMMY GREAVES DURING THE GAME WITH BRAZIL.

Fleet Street they raised a glass to him. Then a bottle. Then another bottle. In fact, their celebrations went on well into the night.

ARSENAL
1975-76

- **League: 17th (Division 1)**
- **FA Cup: 0-3 Wolverhampton Wanderers, round 3**
- **League Cup: 0-1 Everton, round 2 replay**

Bertie Mee always had the air of a benign bank manager. Yet, despite appearing as if he might have been happier discussing interest rate fluctuations than the merits of 4-2-4 over 4-4-2, he more than held his own against hardened football men such as Bill Shankly and Bill Nicholson, and led Arsenal to a historic League and Cup double in 1971. But Bertie struggled with the notoriously difficult 'second album' and

THE ONLY FLAIR IN THE ARSENAL TEAM WAS IN THEIR TROUSERS

by the mid-seventies the only flair in the Arsenal team was in their trousers. Key players like Charlie George, Frank McLintock and Ray Kennedy had gone and not been properly replaced. McLintock's successor in central defence, the amiable, bald, gangling but essentially hapless figure of Terry Mancini, could have been the prototype for Pascal Cygan. The youngsters offered some hope but for every Liam Brady there was a John Matthews. Elsewhere in midfield, hatchet man Peter Storey had reached the age where he had to have a lie-down after kicking an opponent. He prowled the centre circle in the manner

⚽ ODDBALL

ARSENAL FULLBACK SAMMY NELSON RECEIVED A TWO-WEEK SUSPENSION FOR MOONING AT THE HIGHBURY CROWD AFTER SCORING AGAINST COVENTRY IN 1979.

of an old lion stalking a herd of wildebeest. The young and the nimble were too quick for him and escaped unscathed. Only the slow and the infirm were in danger of losing a limb. Throughout his career Storey took no prisoners, although various crimes (including attempting to import pornography) meant that he would later have plenty of opportunity to rectify this oversight.

Arsenal's finishing place of seventeenth was their lowest for over fifty years. They were so bad that even Nick Hornby went to watch them only once. At the end of the season Bertie Mee decided to retire from management. A career in football administration beckoned: figures to balance, filing cabinets to sort. He was in his element.

Arsenal's Peter Storey in a rare action shot from 1975.

TOTTENHAM HOTSPUR

1976-77

⚽ **League: 22nd (Division 1)**
⚽ **FA Cup: 0-1 Cardiff City, round 3**
⚽ **League Cup: 2-3 Wrexham, round 3**

By 1976 Spurs fans were living so far in the past they should have demanded Tony Robinson and the Time Team as managers. Supporters raised on the Bill Nicholson 'Glory Glory' days of the early sixties still expected artistic football and an abundance of goals – and, if they didn't get them within the first minute and a half, they turned on the players with a fury that made an Ian Paisley speech sound like an invitation to tea and scones at the Ritz.

RALPH COATES WAS KNOWN FOR HIS COMBOVER

In fairness they had plenty to moan about in the course of this season. Terry Neill had resigned as manager in June to take over at Arsenal, his first signing being Newcastle's prolific goalscorer Malcolm Macdonald, whom he had originally been hoping to sign for Spurs. First-team coach Keith Burkinshaw took over at White Hart Lane, his principal qualification being that, like Nicholson, he was a dour Yorkshireman, seemingly raised in a world of tin baths, pet ferrets and wi' outside toilet at t'end o' t' moor.

The deceptively slow Martin Chivers left for Switzerland before the start of the

⚽ ODDBALL

IN AN ATTEMPT TO BOOST MORALE IN 1998 BELEAGUERED SPURS MANAGER CHRISTIAN GROSS ANNOUNCED PLANS TO TAKE THE PLAYERS TO THE CIRCUS. IT WAS SAID THAT HE WAS USED TO BEING SURROUNDED BY CLOWNS.

season, to be replaced by Ian Moores who formed a blunt spearhead with Chris Jones. Young Glenn Hoddle was beginning to make his mark while on the wing Spurs could call upon Ralph Coates. Just as Cristiano Ronaldo is known for his stepover, Coates was known for his combover. When in full flight, wisps of hair would trail in Coates's wake like Dr Who's scarf in a wind tunnel. Of course nowadays he would be forced to have his hair cut, lest Robert Pires went tumbling over a strand in the penalty area. But the efforts of Hoddle, Coates, Steve Perryman and a few others were insufficient to stave off the inevitable. Fortunately Burkinshaw was not one to panic. Bottom o' t' table, relegated to t' Second Division for t' first time in nearly thirty years, knocked out o' both cup competitions by lower division opposition? Luxury!

Ralph Coates, complete with his distinctive hairstyle, battles for the ball against West Ham's Billy Jennings.

NEWCASTLE UNITED
1977-78

- ⚽ **League: 21st (Division 1)**
- ⚽ **FA Cup: 1-4 Wrexham, round 4 replay**
- ⚽ **League Cup: 0-2 Millwall, round 2**
- ⚽ **UEFA Cup: 2-5 (aggregate) Bastia, round 2**

When manager Gordon Lee left St James' Park to join Everton in January 1977, the Newcastle players demanded that club coach Richard Dinnis be appointed as his successor. Dinnis was an unusual choice. A former schoolteacher, he had never played League football. But, despite mutterings that he was given the job only because the programme-seller was busy and the tea lady's husband didn't want her working Saturdays,

HONEYMOON PERIODS RARELY LAST LONG IN FOOTBALL

Dinnis guided Newcastle to fifth place and a UEFA Cup spot. Sadly honeymoon periods rarely last long in football. One week Dinnis was still wearing the metaphorical stockings and suspenders, the next there was talk of divorce. For after beating Leeds 3-2 at home in the opening game of the 1977-78 season Newcastle lost ten League games on the bounce. They crashed out of the League Cup to Second Division opposition and their performances led to Newcastle legend Jackie Milburn labelling Dinnis 'a rank amateur'. And when a 3-1 home defeat in November by Bastia brought an early exit from Europe, the one-time geography teacher

The Newcastle team's crossed arms would prove their best defensive move all year.

was sacked for fear that he would soon be consulting the atlas to tell the club coach driver how to get to Mansfield, Chesterfield and Walsall.

His replacement was Bill McGarry, a disciplinarian manager of the old school. If the genial Dinnis was Mr Chips, McGarry was the Demon Headmaster. The ex-Ipswich and Wolves boss had been coaching in South Africa but the lure of Wallsend in winter proved impossible to resist. He soon came to realize that swimming with Great White Sharks off Cape Town would have been a picnic next to shoring up Newcastle's leaky defence, a four-goal humiliation in the Cup by Third Division Wrexham merely underlining the problem.

At the other end of the pitch new £150,000 Scottish forward Mark McGhee struggled for goals, so to stop the crowd abusing McGhee for being the worst player

⚽ ODDBALL

FORMER NEWCASTLE KEEPER JOHN BURRIDGE LOVED THE GAME SO MUCH THAT HE USED TO WATCH *MATCH OF THE DAY* IN HIS FULL GOALKEEPING KIT. HE WAS EVEN KNOWN TO TAKE A BALL TO BED AT NIGHT AND, TO THE DISMAY OF HIS WIFE, CONDUCT IMAGINARY POST-MATCH INTERVIEWS WITH GERALD SINSTADT IN HIS SLEEP.

in the team McGarry signed Mike Larnach. Relegation had long been inevitable and the Magpies finished ten points adrift of safety. Those halcyon days of winning the Texaco Cup two years in succession were now just a distant memory.

Scotland
1978 WORLD CUP FINALS

From the moment it began you just knew it was going to end in disappointment and discord. Yes, 'Ally's Tartan Army' by Scottish comedian Andy Cameron really was that bad. Week after week he occupied a valuable three minutes on *Top of the Pops*, at the expense of Blondie and The Stranglers, warbling about how Scotland were going to win the World Cup because they 'were the greatest football team'. It made you long for Clive Dunn to record a follow-up to 'Grandad'. And, as predictions go, Cameron's ditty was right up there with Chamberlain's 'peace in our time' and Custer's 'Indians? What Indians?'.

THAT GREAT PANTOMIME TRADITION, THE SCOTTISH GOALKEEPER

Although the first to put it into 'song', Cameron wasn't responsible for the original notion that victory in Argentina was a mere formality for the Scots. That honour went to manager Ally MacLeod. A cartoonist's dream who became a supporter's nightmare, good old Ally vowed to succeed where other Scottish bosses had failed by moulding a bunch of great players (well, Kenny Dalglish) into a team that looked as if it had been together for years instead of one that appeared to be on a blind date. Even though that great pantomime tradition, the

Scottish goalkeeper (in this case, Alan Rough), was always liable to snatch defeat from the jaws of victory, Ally was supremely confident. But soon he was walking about as tall as the entrants in a Jimmy Krankie lookalike contest. After a 3-1 mauling at the hands of Peru in the opening group game, Ally thought things couldn't get any worse. Then winger Willie Johnston, sent off twenty-one times in his career, found a new way of making an early exit by failing a dope test. 'Pep pills?' queried the shell-shocked tartan army. 'We thought they were tranquillizers!' An own-goal earned a 1-1 draw against mighty Iran but, despite Archie Gemmill weaving through the Dutch defence like a cross between Franz Klammer and PacMan, a 3-2 win in the final group

⚽ **ODDBALL**

APPROACHED BY A STRAY DOG IN ARGENTINA, THE BELEAGUERED ALLY MACLEOD PATTED THE ANIMAL ON THE HEAD, SAYING: 'YOU, MY OLD SON, MAY BE THE ONLY FRIEND I HAVE LEFT IN THE WORLD.' THE DOG PROMPTLY BIT HIS HAND.

game wasn't enough to send the Scots through. Ally returned home to national derision but safe in the knowledge that the answer to the question, 'What do you call a Scotsman in the second round of the World Cup?' remained the same … 'Ref!'

You could have offered Ally MacLeod a penny for his thoughts and still got change.

CHELSEA
1978-79

- ⚽ **League: 22nd (Division 1)**
- ⚽ **FA Cup: 0-3 Manchester United, round 3**
- ⚽ **League Cup: 1-2 Bolton, round 2**

By the summer of 1978 the swinging Chelsea of Charlie Cooke, Alan Hudson, Ian Hutchinson and Peter Osgood were, rather like threepenny bits, jamboree bags and Hughie Green's career, consigned to the past. The exciting players that had lit up the London scene had been replaced by functional, cut-price performers. Instead of trendy King's Road boutiques Chelsea were now browsing in their local pound shop. True, Osgood was still there after a fashion, having returned to Stamford Bridge from the US, but he would make only nine League appearances during the 1978-79 season. Peter Bonetti, too, was still around but 'The Cat' was now about as athletic as Bagpuss and was replaced by Yugoslav international keeper Petar Borota. The only other survivor from the old Chelsea set was Ron 'Chopper' Harris and, let's be honest, it would have needed a manager with a death wish to tell Ron Harris that his time was up. Among the newcomers Gary Stanley, John Sitton and Micky Nutton tried in vain to make a virtue out of running about a lot. Young Ray

'THE CAT' WAS NOW ABOUT AS ATHLETIC AS BAGPUSS

☻ ODDBALL

CHELSEA GOALKEEPER DAVE BEASANT MISSED THE START OF THE 1993-94 SEASON AFTER DROPPING A JAR OF SALAD CREAM ON HIS BIG TOE.

Wilkins was a rapidly emerging talent but, as with the little boy in the park who says 'I'll only play if my brother can play too', a starting place also had to be found for Ray's sibling Graham. Kylie Minogue must have sympathized with Chelsea's plight.

With five League wins and ninety-two goals conceded (including a 7-2 drubbing at Middlesbrough), Chelsea unsurprisingly finished rock bottom. Ex-player Ken Shellito had started the season in charge and was allowed to fork out £165,000 on striker Duncan McKenzie – who repaid the faith with just four goals. Shellito was duly sacked and, after famous Yugoslav coach Miljan Miljanic turned down the post, the board in desperation turned to Danny Blanchflower, who had been out of active football for fifteen years and was earning his living reporting on the game for a national newspaper. It was like asking James Whittaker to become Queen. The board's confidence in their new man can be gauged by the fact that he was appointed on a month-to-month basis. A deep thinker, Blanchflower did little to enhance his reputation during his short spell at Chelsea. One senior player said of him: 'He is fascinating to listen to but we're never quite sure what he's trying to say!' A career in business management surely beckoned.

Chelsea goalkeeper Peter Bonetti. Both the player and pitch had seen better days.

BLACKBURN ROVERS
1978-79

⚽ **League: 22nd (Division 2)**
⚽ **FA Cup: 0-1 Liverpool, round 4**
⚽ **League Cup: 1-2 Exeter City, round 2**

For the residents of the *Coronation Street*-style terraced houses that bordered Ewood Park, supporting Rovers had become something of a chore. Indeed, Albert Tatlock still had a paper round the last time Blackburn won the League title. And in recent seasons the team had flitted between the Second and Third Divisions. There was more chance of finding the crew of the *Marie Celeste* sharing a flat with Glenn Miller and the Surrey puma than of

QUASIMODO HAD GREATER PULLING POWER THAN BLACKBURN

recapturing Blackburn's glory days. A finishing position of fifth in 1978 had, however, given cause for guarded optimism in a part of the world not known for extravagant statements. To this day some locals remain unsure as to whether electricity will ever catch on. Manager Jim Iley decided to build on the previous season by recruiting experience in the shape of ex-Arsenal striker John Radford and former Manchester United forward John Aston, but these signings were offset by the departure to Blackpool, on the eve of the season, of popular winger Dave Wagstaffe. The fans blamed Iley for Wagstaffe's exit

✪ ODDBALL

THE PARTY PIECE OF BLACKBURN'S WOULD-BE STRIKER DUNCAN MCKENZIE WAS VAULTING OVER MINI CARS. HE WAS ALSO AN ACCOMPLISHED JUGGLER AND COULD THROW A GOLF BALL FROM ONE END OF THE GROUND TO THE OTHER.

and, when Stoke City striker Dave Gregory chose to join Third Division Bury in preference to Rovers, it became apparent that even Quasimodo had greater pulling power than Blackburn. After a poor start to the 1978-79 season produced a solitary win from eight League games, Iley brought in two more strikers – Joe Craig from Celtic for

Striker Duncan McKenzie came from Chelsea to the Rovers, billed as the star to save them from the drop. As it happened he was a rather feeble flop.

£40,000 and another veteran, Alan Birchenall, from Memphis Rogues. Such was the average age of the team that most of the players were more familiar with a bus pass than a back pass. But within forty-eight hours of the double signing Iley was sacked after less than six months in charge.

Iley's assistant John Pickering was appointed caretaker manager, helped out by Radford. Displaying the vision of Mr Magoo, the board upgraded Pickering to manager in February 1979, in the middle of a club record sequence of sixteen games without a victory. With goals still as rare as an outbreak of crowd surfing at a Daniel O'Donnell concert, the board splashed out £80,000 on yet another forward, Chelsea's Duncan McKenzie – a deal financed by the sale of Kevin Hird to Leeds for £375,000. A showman both on and off the pitch, McKenzie had acquired a reputation for promising more than he delivered and many fans thought he belonged in a circus rather than a football club. They feared that the quickest way to kill the team's chances was to go for the juggler. They were right. McKenzie's arrival did nothing to halt the decline and a 3-1 home defeat to Newcastle on 25 April saw Blackburn relegated with four games still to play. Pickering's contract was not renewed. Fortunately for these Rovers, the name of one licensee at Weatherfield's most famous pub would, a decade or so later, lay down a blueprint for a brighter future. Equally fortunately it was Jack Walker and not Bet Lynch.

MANCHESTER CITY

1979-80

- ☺ **League: 17th (Division 1)**
- ☺ **FA Cup: 0-1 Halifax Town, round 3**
- ☺ **League Cup: 0-1 Sunderland, round 3 replay**

Malcolm Allison: you either loathed him or you tolerated him. Outstanding as a coach at Maine Road under Joe Mercer, the flamboyant Allison (only Monica Lewinsky has done more to popularize cigars) was an altogether different proposition in his two spells as City manager. Lacking the presence of a wise old head to curb his excesses, Big Mal was allowed to run wild, wheeling and dealing in the market like Del

ONLY MONICA LEWINSKY HAS DONE MORE TO POPULARIZE CIGARS

Boy and Rodney but without their innate business sense. During his second stint in charge from 1979 to 1980 Allison got rid of popular players such as Brian Kidd, Dave Watson, Gary Owen, Peter Barnes and Asa Hartford and replaced them with headline-grabbing, big-money buys. Midfielder Steve Daley joined from Wolves for a then British record fee of £1,437,500 in September 1979, followed six months later by the arrival of striker Kevin Reeves from Norwich for £1,250,000. The pair quickly became the talk of Manchester … in the same way that Eddie the Eagle would become the talk of ski jumping.

⚽ ODDBALL

IN 1995 A MANCHESTER CITY FAN WAS BANNED FROM TAKING DEAD CHICKENS INTO THE MAINE ROAD GROUND. HE USED TO CELEBRATE A CITY GOAL BY SWINGING THE BIRD AROUND HIS HEAD.

City's form throughout the season was wretched. At one stage Allison's men went seventeen games without a win. Even Alastair Campbell might have struggled to put a positive spin on that. In the end they were relieved to finish above the relegation zone. But it was in the FA Cup that they really excelled themselves, crashing out ignominiously to Fourth Division Halifax Town. The fans still chanted Allison's name but it was usually followed by the word 'out'. The world of football was just grateful that Arthur Cox was never subjected to similar chants for his dismissal. Allison was duly sacked early the following season.

Manager Malcolm Allison. The hat, coat and team tactics all screamed 'dick' – in the 'private investigator' sense of the word, of course.

CRYSTAL PALACE

1980-81

- ⚽ **League: 22nd (Division 1)**
- ⚽ **FA Cup: 0-4 Manchester City, round 3**
- ⚽ **League Cup: 1-3 Tottenham Hotspur, round 3 replay**

All clubs cite bad luck at some stage but to have both Terry Venables and Malcolm Allison as your manager in the same season goes way beyond bad luck. It is the stuff of conspiracy theories. Things were so bad that Gypsy women selling sprigs of lucky heather in Oxford Street were known to take one look at the red and blue Palace scarf, shake their heads knowingly and move on. Even the Samaritans hung up on Palace fans. Yet at the start of the season there had been great optimism around Selhurst Park. Venables had recently declared that Palace would be the team of the eighties and he was right … if you also consider Neil Kinnock to have been the politician of the eighties.

During the summer of 1980 Venables had swapped Palace fullback Kenny Sansom for Arsenal's teenage striker Clive Allen, pairing the latter in attack with Mike Flanagan. Always fancying himself as a bit of a singer, Venables had been unable to resist a partnership of Flanagan and Allen. Sadly they played more like Laurel and Hardy. After a run of seven straight League defeats and with a

EVEN THE SAMARITANS HUNG UP ON PALACE FANS

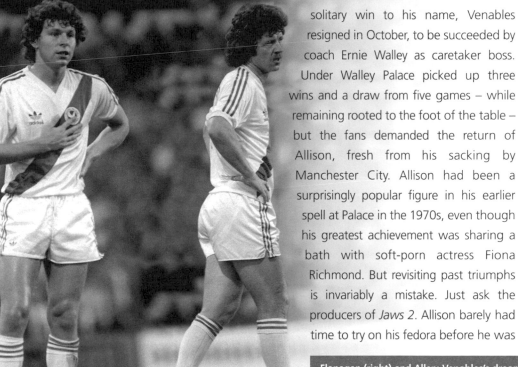

solitary win to his name, Venables resigned in October, to be succeeded by coach Ernie Walley as caretaker boss. Under Walley Palace picked up three wins and a draw from five games – while remaining rooted to the foot of the table – but the fans demanded the return of Allison, fresh from his sacking by Manchester City. Allison had been a surprisingly popular figure in his earlier spell at Palace in the 1970s, even though his greatest achievement was sharing a bath with soft-porn actress Fiona Richmond. But revisiting past triumphs is invariably a mistake. Just ask the producers of *Jaws 2*. Allison barely had time to try on his fedora before he was

Flanagan (right) and Allen: Venables's dream team. They played more like Laurel and Hardy.

⚽ ODDBALL

CRYSTAL PALACE MISSED OUT ON PROMOTION FROM THE THIRD DIVISION IN 1976 AFTER HYPNOTIST ROMARK, WHO HAD FALLEN OUT WITH MANAGER MALCOLM ALLISON, CLAIMED TO HAVE PUT A CURSE ON THE TEAM.

sacked after two months with just one win to his name. New chairman Ron Noades wanted to rebuild Palace in the image of Wimbledon, which was a bit like dumping a rusty old shed in the garden of a smart suburban semi. So he appointed former Dons boss Dario Gradi as Palace's fourth manager that season. Gradi fared no better than his predecessors, presiding over a run of seven successive defeats before Palace finally picked up their first win of 1981, against Birmingham, in April. But by then the writing had been on the wall so long it was in hieroglyphics. Palace were relegated with nineteen points. The board quickly realized that what they really needed was a new manager …

CHELSEA
1982-83

- League: 18th (Division 2)
- FA Cup: 1-2 Derby County, round 4
- League Cup: 0-2 Notts County, round 3

After two seasons of mid-table mediocrity manager John Neal vowed to get Chelsea out of the Second Division. He very nearly did … by taking them down to the Third. With relegation a distinct possibility until the first week in May, this season marked the lowest point in Chelsea's history – lower even than the release of 'Blue Is The Colour'. Under new owner Ken Bates these were dark days. The big summer signing was thirty-seven-year-old Bryan 'Pop' Robson, a

THE LOWEST POINT IN CHELSEA'S HISTORY

fine player in his time but by 1982 his talent had receded as far as his hairline. Colin Lee, in his pre-bouffant days, led the attack alongside that fiery little scamp David Speedie. Some managers treated Speedie with kid gloves but others used rubber ones because he was such an irritant. In midfield Mike Fillery's silky skills were often hard to detect on cold evenings in Barnsley, Grimsby or Rotherham, while the fans never really took to winger Peter Rhoades-Brown, possibly because his name was so difficult to chant. 'Give us a hyphen' doesn't really have that ring to it. The one reassuring figure was long-serving, giant central defender Micky Droy, who was probably still around only because nobody could move him off the pitch.

With floating fans deciding that a sixth series of *Terry and June* offered more appeal than a trip to the Bridge, attendances dropped alarmingly. Only 7,808 turned up to see the biggest win of the season – a 6-0 hammering of Cambridge United. Neal kept promising a stirring finish but one win in the final eleven games left Chelsea needing a fortuitous goal from Clive Walker at Bolton to provide the victory that guaranteed safety. Yet within a year Chelsea would be striding back to the top flight. If you had suggested that to fans in May 1983 they would have said it was about as likely as the club one day being taken over by a Russian multi-billionaire with a strange dummy-like grin.

⚽ ODDBALL

BEFORE MAKING HIS SENIOR DEBUT, CHELSEA DEFENDER CELESTINE BABAYARO WAS RULED OUT FOR SIX WEEKS AT THE START OF THE 1997-98 SEASON WITH A STRESS ANKLE FRACTURE ... SUSTAINED DURING ACROBATIC CELEBRATIONS TO MARK A GOAL IN A RESERVE TEAM FRIENDLY AT STEVENAGE.

Defender Micky Droy appeals to his teammates to show some semblance of talent.

DERBY COUNTY
1983-84

- ⚽ **League: 20th (Division 2)**
- ⚽ **FA Cup: 0-1 Plymouth Argyle, round 6 replay**
- ⚽ **League Cup: 0-7 (aggregate) Birmingham City, round 2**

Just as the words 'Crazy Frog' strike terror into parents in 2005, so another name sent shivers down the spines of football supporters in the 1980s: Robert Maxwell. The media mogul was on his world domination tour, part of which seemed to involve buying every football club in the land. With the same inevitability of a Dennis Waterman theme song, whenever a club was up for sale Maxwell would appear on the scene, waving his wad. He already owned Oxford United and, when he failed in a bid to take over Manchester United, he turned his attention to ailing Derby. Less than a decade after being crowned League champions Derby were in a sorry state, the board's mastery of finances equal only to Old Mother Hubbard's grasp of housekeeping. They were £1.5m in debt and faced with a winding-up notice on account of £129,000 owed to the Inland Revenue. No wonder the world's fattest vulture was circling overhead.

DERBY WERE IN A SORRY STATE

Sadly for the fans events on the pitch were equally gloomy. Peter Taylor had returned to his old stamping ground in sole charge but he and Brian Clough were never as effective when separated. Taylor needed someone to bounce off. In that respect, at least, Maxwell should have been ideal. There was rancour even before the season started with Taylor snatching influential winger John Robertson from Clough's Nottingham Forest for £135,000 – a move that sparked a bitter feud between Clough and Taylor. In the event Robertson spent most of his time at Derby injured. The opening game of the campaign saw a 5-0 defeat at Chelsea (Blackburn and Barnsley would also put five past Derby in the course of the season) and, as unrest spread in the dressing room, Taylor bluntly told veteran midfielder Archie Gemmill that his legs had gone. While the search went on for Gemmill's legs, things got so bad that Taylor was given a vote of confidence, a move that is usually tantamount to giving a condemned man a hearty breakfast. When Derby were drawn against non-League Telford in the fourth round of the FA Cup, Taylor claimed that his side were the underdogs. Few disagreed. Derby scraped through 3-2 in controversial fashion, but hopes of a lucrative Cup run were dashed by a blunder from goalkeeper Steve Cherry in the sixth round against Third Division Plymouth. A fire sale of players and a little help from Maxwell eventually staved off the winding-up order but results, which relied heavily on the goals of Bobby Davison,

⚽ ODDBALL

DERBY'S FIRST GAME AT THEIR NEW PRIDE PARK STADIUM IN 1997 CAME TO A PREMATURE FINISH WHEN THE FLOODLIGHTS FAILED AFTER FIFTY-FIVE MINUTES. DERBY WERE LEADING WIMBLEDON 2-1 AT THE TIME.

did not improve and in April Taylor was summoned by the new board. Earlier in the season he had vowed: 'I won't pack it in. They will have to shoot me to get rid of me.' Now the only debate was whether the club could afford a blindfold for the execution. Following Taylor's dismissal, his assistant Roy McFarland took over – but the appointment was too late to stave off relegation.

Although Maxwell had helped to keep the club in business, the absentee chairman was hardly popular with Derby fans who over the coming seasons chanted joyously: 'He's fat, he's round, he's never at the ground…' And given Maxwell's habit of misappropriating funds, you couldn't help but wonder whether it was he who had taken Archie Gemmill's legs …

The Derby money-man Robert Maxwell. As the fans succinctly sang, 'He's fat, he's round, he's never at the ground…'

WOLVERHAMPTON WANDERERS

1984-85

- ☺ **League: 22nd (Division 2)**
- ☺ **FA Cup: 1-3 Huddersfield, round 3 replay**
- ☺ **League Cup: 0-2 Southampton, round 3 replay**

When Tommy Docherty took over as manager of relegated Wolves in June 1984 the Molineux fans probably didn't know whether to laugh or cry. After all, his CV has always been a mix of creative brilliance and destructive farce. Think Johann Strauss crossed with Norman Wisdom and you'll get the general idea. He was equally capable of leading teams to the Promised Land or the Conference. His biggest problem

A MIX OF CREATIVE BRILLIANCE AND DESTRUCTIVE FARCE

seemed to be a habit of tinkering with perfection. At Chelsea in the sixties his detractors accused him of dismantling – for no apparent reason – the buoyant young team he had created. When he departed to Australia in 1981, it was rumoured that the first thing he did was redesign the kangaroo with the pouch at the back. At least with Docherty at the helm there's never a dull moment, the wisecracks invariably flowing faster than the goals.

At Molineux he inherited a team that was short on confidence and a club that was even shorter on money and living on past glories. Docherty said that when he opened the trophy cabinet two Japanese prisoners of war came out. Although there was precious little cash for wheeling and dealing, the Doc, in typical fashion, managed to bring in no fewer than eighteen new players during the season. He was able to field experienced professionals such as Geoff Palmer, John Humphrey and Alan Ainscow alongside promising youngsters like Tim Flowers and John Pender. The early indications were that Docherty might be able to steady the ship and after three months Wolves sat a comfortable thirteenth in the table … but then a 5-1 drubbing at Grimsby started the rot. After a 2-1 success at Fulham on 24 November the next victory was at Carlisle on 8 April – twenty games later. At one point they scored just one goal in 963 minutes of

Wolves' boss Tommy Docherty: he could always see the funny side – they were in black and gold.

League football. As Docherty quipped: 'We don't use a stopwatch to judge our golden

goal competition now. We use a calendar.'

Wolves finished bottom – seven points from safety – and the grand old club was relegated to the Third Division for the first time in over sixty years. Gates had plummeted from the 15,000 that saw the season's opener against Sheffield United to fewer than 4,500, the turnout for the final home game against Huddersfield. There were so many empty spaces on the terraces that fans communicated with the person next to them by semaphore. As it happened Wolves beat Huddersfield 2-1 to record their first triumph at Molineux since early November. The financial crisis at the club had already claimed the thinning scalp of chief executive Derek Dougan in January and it came as no surprise when Docherty followed him out of the door at the end of the season. But for Wolves the nightmare was far from over. They were

⚽ ODDBALL

IN NOVEMBER 1998 WOLFIE, THE WOLVES MASCOT, WAS INVOLVED IN A SURREAL HALF-TIME PUNCH-UP WITH THREE LITTLE PIGS AT BRISTOL CITY'S ASHTON GATE GROUND. THE PIGS WERE HOSTING A CHILDREN'S PENALTY SHOOT-OUT TO PROMOTE A DOUBLE-GLAZING FIRM BUT, WHEN TEMPERS BECAME FRAYED, ONE OF THE PIGS AIMED A TROTTER AT WOLFIE. AS STEWARDS INTERVENED, WOLFIE WAS ACCUSED OF GIVING THE PIG A CUT LIP. A POLICE SPOKESMAN SAID OF THE INCIDENT: 'THERE WAS A LOT OF HUFFING AND PUFFING.'

relegated again the following season, thus dropping from the First Division to the Fourth in three inglorious years. In terms of a fall from grace the Hamiltons had nothing on Wolves.

BIRMINGHAM CITY
1985-86

- **League: 21st (Division 1)**
- **FA Cup: 1-2 Altrincham, round 3**
- **League Cup: 0-3 Southampton, round 3 replay**

Back in the early eighties when law and order were taken seriously, persistent offenders were sent to one of three institutions – Parkhurst, Wormwood Scrubs or St Andrew's. Of these the last named, home of Birmingham City FC, was by far the toughest. Only the real hard cases were sent there – guys like Mick Harford, Julian Dicks, Martin Kuhl and Robert Hopkins. It was said they would nail a teammate's head to the dressing-room door just for underhitting a back pass or taking a last Rolo. Such was the reputation of these men for carrying out GBH on the pitch that players from other clubs used to dread getting a close-season call from the governor, Ron Saunders, making them an offer they couldn't refuse. The Krays deliberately pretended to be crap at football just so they wouldn't be sent to St Andrew's. By the summer of 1985 Harford had been released on parole, leaving Dicks and Kuhl to control the main block while Hopkins, in the number 11 shirt, was out on A Wing.

KNOCKED OUT OF THE CUP BY NON-LEAGUE ALTRINCHAM

A man who smiled only at coronations, Saunders had even fewer reasons to be cheerful that season. The Birmingham enforcers were struggling to leave their mark on the opposition and when, with a young David Seaman in goal, they were knocked out of the Cup by non-League Altrincham, Saunders was fired. His replacement, John Bond, was always remembered by fans long after he had left their club. Indeed in 1992 Burnley supporters were so keen to chat to him about old times that Bond had to watch his new club Shrewsbury's visit to Turf Moor disguised as a steward for fear of reprisals. Bond's first game in charge at St Andrew's brought a 1-0 win over Oxford – City's first victory since September – but it proved a false dawn. Bond said they'd turned the corner; the fans would have been happy just to win a corner. In the end only one team finished below Birmingham – neighbours

⚽ ODDBALL

BIRMINGHAM CITY DIDN'T COMPETE IN THE 1921-22 FA CUP … BECAUSE THE CLUB FORGOT TO POST THE ENTRY FORM.

West Brom whose new manager was … Ron Saunders. He thus had the distinction of presiding over the relegation of two teams in one season. For one year, at least, crime didn't pay.

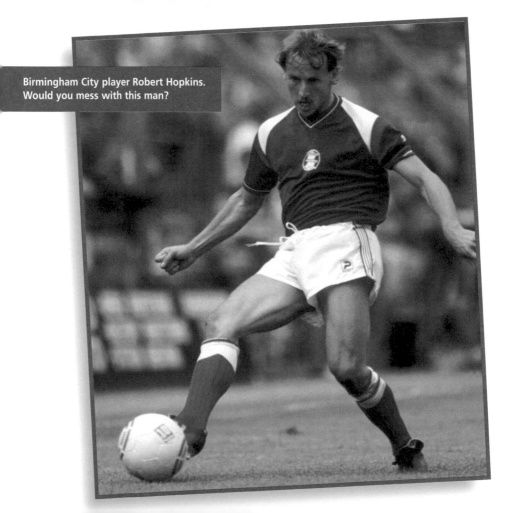
Birmingham City player Robert Hopkins.
Would you mess with this man?

GLASGOW RANGERS

1985-86

- ☻ **League: 5th (Scottish Premier Division)**
- ☻ **Scottish FA Cup: 2-3 Hearts, round 3**
- ☻ **Scottish League Cup: 0-1 Hibernian, semi-final**
- ☻ **UEFA Cup: 1-2 (aggregate) Atletico Osasuna, round 1**

Jock Wallace first made Rangers players sick in 1967 when, as goalkeeper for little Berwick Rangers, he starred in the greatest giant-killing in the history of the Scottish Cup, when the minnows beat the Glasgow team 1-0. When he became manager at Ibrox in the 1970s he made the Rangers players sick again by forcing them to run up and down dunes in pre-season training. An ex-Army man whose love of discipline might have made him an ideal client for Cynthia Payne, Wallace led Rangers to two trebles. Although by Glasgow standards that's not much to drink, the fans loved him. He returned to the club for a second spell in the eighties and, while he still made Vlad the Impaler look like Julian Clary, he found it hard to repeat his earlier success. By the 1985-86 season Rangers hadn't won the League since 1978 or the Cup since 1981. And in Scotland that's almost as big a crime as taking a collection box … and putting money in it. The only consolation was that for the past

WALLACE MADE VLAD THE IMPALER LOOK LIKE JULIAN CLARY

two seasons Alex Ferguson's Aberdeen had prevented Celtic getting *their* hands on the League title. But with Celtic now battling it out with Hearts at the top and Rangers, who relied solely on the goals of Ally McCoist, languishing in mid-table, the knives were out for Wallace. He could have sharpened them on his tongue but instead, in April 1986 – the day after Rangers lost to Spurs in a friendly at Ibrox – he took one between the shoulder blades. Big Jock was on his way, to be replaced by another man not exactly from the Perry Como school of management, Graeme Souness.

Rangers finished the season with thirty-five points from thirty-six games – their lowest-ever tally. To add insult to injury, Celtic pipped Hearts for the title. To Rangers fans it was like your boss running off with your wife and then coming back to tell you what a great shag she was. Only worse.

⚽ ODDBALL

AFTER MISSING A SITTER AGAINST ABERDEEN IN 1991, RANGERS' CONTROVERSIAL STRIKER MO JOHNSTON WAS SO ANGRY WITH HIMSELF THAT HE PICKED UP A PIECE OF MUD AND HURLED IT TO THE GROUND. IN DOING SO, HE INJURED HIS BACK AND WAS FORCED TO MISS THE NEXT MATCH.

Rangers' goalie Chris Woods makes a rare save, in a season which saw the Scottish giants accrue just thirty-five points from thirty-six games.

MANCHESTER UNITED
1986-87

- **League: 11th (Division 1)**
- **FA Cup: 0-1 Coventry City, round 4**
- **League Cup: 1-4 Southampton, round 4 replay**

After sacking Ron Atkinson in November 1986 in the wake of League Cup humiliation by Southampton, the United board reckoned they needed a quieter, more thoughtful, self-effacing manager, someone who could keep out of the headlines. So naturally they chose Alex Ferguson.

Back in the days when a pizza in the face would have changed his complexion, Fergie arrived at Old Trafford claiming that the League could still be won.

FERGIE ARRIVED CLAIMING THAT THE LEAGUE COULD STILL BE WON

What he failed to add was 'by Everton'. In fact, United finished thirty points adrift of the champions and below such superpowers as Wimbledon, Luton and Watford. Fergie was not helped by a strike force that even Arthur Scargill would have rejected. Mark Hughes had been sold to Barcelona in pre-season and his replacement, Peter Davenport, was already drawing unfavourable comparisons with another costly import from Nottingham Forest, Garry Birtles, who had failed to score in his first twenty-five league games for United in 1980-81. Frank Stapleton was nearing his sell-by date and Terry Gibson was, frankly,

⚽ ODDBALL

UNITED KEEPER ALEX STEPNEY SPENT SO MUCH TIME SHOUTING AT HIS TEAMMATES DURING A 1975 GAME WITH BIRMINGHAM CITY THAT HE WAS TAKEN TO HOSPITAL WITH A DISLOCATED JAW.

short. When defenders talked of having him in their pocket, it wasn't necessarily a metaphor. Meanwhile in midfield Bryan Robson's shoulder was always likely to drop off at any minute.

Fortunately Fergie had an excuse for the team's indifferent form – the club's new £80,000 undersoil heating system which, to use the correct technical terminology, didn't work. Appearing to have been installed by the Chuckle Brothers, it left parts of the Old Trafford pitch as hard as a politician's heart and, when United were dumped out of the FA Cup by Coventry after the ball bobbled away from keeper Chris Turner on the slippery surface, it was the heating system that bore the brunt of Fergie's fury. That summer it was ripped out and has never been invited back to Old Trafford, not even for eighties' nights or testimonials. But it did mean that Fergie would have to come up with a fresh excuse when things went wrong. Just as he was racking his brains, the kit man passed and said: 'What do you reckon to grey shirts, boss?'

Man United boss Alex Ferguson – cocky as ever, but his team finished below such superpowers as Wimbledon, Luton and Watford in the 1986-87 season.

SUNDERLAND
1986-87

- **League: 20th (Division 2)**
- **FA Cup: 1-2 Wimbledon, round 3**
- **League Cup: 5-5 (lost on away goals) York City, round 1**

By 1986 Sunderland FC was not just a sleeping giant, it was practically comatose. Apart from the memorable FA Cup triumph of 1973, the once proud club had underachieved since the days when *Gone with the Wind* was showing at the local Gaumont. But this season would be worse than even the most pessimistic of fans could have feared, and would see Sunderland fall into the Third Division for the first time in

THE THIRD DIVISION FOR THE FIRST TIME IN THEIR HISTORY

their history. Yet the early omens were good and at the end of October the club were lying fifth. But then performances began to drop off faster than the front row at a Roger Whittaker concert.

In January manager Lawrie McMenemy agreed to take a sizeable pay cut but, despite the presence of experienced players such as George Burley, Eric Gates and Dave Swindlehurst, results failed to improve. A change of leadership was inevitable. Sunderland legend Bob Stokoe tried to work his old magic in a caretaker capacity but it would have needed Paul Daniels (assisted by the lovely Debbie

McGee) to get the club out of this mess. By finishing in twentieth position Sunderland entered the lottery of the newly introduced play-offs, where they went out on away goals to Gillingham and were relegated. Things were shabbier than Stokoe's famous raincoat. Meanwhile the board were at their wits' end. For some members it had not been a long journey.

⚽ ODDBALL

SUNDERLAND FAN STEPHEN JONES DESERTED HIS VERY NEW WIFE TO WATCH HIS TEAM PLAY GRIMSBY IN 1998-99. HE LEFT THE WEDDING RECEPTION AT WINGATE, COUNTY DURHAM, AND ORDERED THE LIMOUSINE CHAUFFEUR TO DRIVE HIM, HIS BEST MAN AND THE USHERS TO THE STADIUM OF LIGHT. ANOTHER TWENTY-EIGHT GUESTS FOLLOWED IN A MINI-BUS. BUOYED BY A 3-1 WIN, HE RETURNED TO THE RECEPTION – AND HIS UNDERSTANDING BRIDE – AFTER THE GAME.

Caretaker manager Bob Stokoe has every right to look shifty as he oversees the demise of Sunderland in their worst-ever season.

TOTTENHAM HOTSPUR
1987-88

- ⚽ **League: 13th (Division 1)**
- ⚽ **FA Cup: 1-2 Port Vale, round 4**
- ⚽ **League Cup: 1-2 Aston Villa, round 3**

Rather like Dennis Bergkamp certain London teams have not always travelled well. On a boggy pitch any northern side used to fancy their chances against West Ham or their equally cultured capital cousins. So, when Spurs were drawn to visit Port Vale in the FA Cup at the end of January 1988, alarm bells started ringing. Vale may have been languishing in eighteenth place in Division Three but the pitch was sure to be stickier than a teenage boy's

AN INAUSPICIOUS START FOR NEW MANAGER TERRY VENABLES

copy of *Knave*. And the word on the streets was that Spurs did not like it up 'em. This was an occasion that called for a bear of a man and in their line-up Spurs had a player who fitted that description. Chris Waddle was indeed a bear, but only in the sense that he hibernated in winter. When the going got muddy, you would rather have had Edmund Blackadder with you in the trenches than Waddle. At the other extreme Spurs could call upon Neil Ruddock who, even at that tender age, was bulky enough to warrant diversion signs whenever he fell over.

Spurs' predictable defeat capped an

inauspicious start for new manager Terry Venables, fresh from topping up his tan in Barcelona. Beaten Cup finalists the previous season, Spurs had lost Glenn Hoddle to Monaco in the summer and manager David Pleat to the tabloids in October, following lurid allegations about his one-man crusade to make Luton worth visiting.

Venables's response to the subsequent slump was to sign goalkeeper Bobby Mimms, striker Paul Walsh and, naturally, Terry Fenwick, a recurring theme of his management career. In the same way that an alcoholic orders another drink, Venables would send for Terry Fenwick. He also jettisoned two of Pleat's last signings, the ex-Forest pair of Chris Fairclough and Dutchman Johnny Metgod (pronounced 'Met-hod', which must have been confusing for Amsterdam churchgoers). Alas, Spurs fans could no longer worship their own Hod

⚽ ODDBALL

SPURS FORWARDS LES FERDINAND AND RUEL FOX MISSED THE START OF THE SECOND HALF AT NEWCASTLE IN 1997 AFTER GETTING THEMSELVES LOCKED IN THE TOILET.

and, without Glenn's artistry, the team struggled. Luckily El Tel promised a brighter future. But didn't he always?

Goalkeeper Bobby Mimms, pointing the way to where Spurs' hopes went.

PORTSMOUTH

1987-88

⚽ **League:** 19th (Division 1)
⚽ **FA Cup:** 1-3 Luton Town, round 6
⚽ **League Cup:** 2-6 (aggregate) Swindon Town, round 2

The history of football is littered with truly great players who have struggled as managers – Billy Wright, Bobby Moore, Bobby Charlton, er … Trevor Francis. To that list has to be added Alan Ball, a genuine enthusiast whose tendency to wear his heart on his sleeve amazed fans and doctors alike. Bally did enjoy the occasional triumph – such as guiding Portsmouth to the Second Division title in 1987 – but as sure as night follows day, his success would be followed almost immediately by disaster. Maybe part of the reason lay with the fact that, because of his high-pitched voice, only dogs could hear his pre-match instructions.

After leading Pompey back to the top flight for the first time in twenty-eight years, Ball's feet hardly touched the ground. A set of lower chairs helped but it soon became apparent that the team was ill equipped for the task in hand. They would have been out of their depth in the shallow end of the local swimming pool. The attack was led by thirty-four-year-old Paul Mariner and Micky 'Sumo' Quinn – who was to

SUCCESS WOULD BE FOLLOWED IMMEDIATELY BY DISASTER

⚽ ODDBALL

IN 1994 PORTSMOUTH FAN MIKE HALL SAID HE WAS GOING TO SUE THE LEAGUE FOR HIS TICKET MONEY AND TRAVEL COSTS FOR WHAT HE CLAIMED WAS A WASTED TRIP TO OLDHAM TO SEE POMPEY BEATEN BY TWO DISPUTED PENALTIES.

dieting what Brian Sewell is to army camouflage trousers. In fact the sight of Quinn is believed to have inspired the terrace craze for inflatables. To bolster his strike force Ball recruited Ian Baird from Leeds for £385,000 but, when the opening game at Fratton Park ended in a 3-0 defeat to Chelsea, and two matches later Pompey were mauled 6-0 at Highbury, it indicated a long winter ahead.

Off the field the club's assets were temporarily frozen by the bank, forcing chairman John Deacon to pay the players out of his own pocket. He must have been tempted to put the money to better use – such as on the 2.30 at Catterick. A closing run of one win in thirteen condemned Portsmouth to a quick return to Division Two, but Ball was always assured of a warm welcome in the city. Then again, so was Joan of Arc at Rouen.

Even Ian Baird's impressive acrobatic displays weren't enough to save Portsmouth from relegation.

NEWCASTLE UNITED
1988-89

- ⚽ **League: 20th (Division 1)**
- ⚽ **FA Cup: 0-1 Watford, round 3**
- ⚽ **League Cup: 2-4 (aggregate) Southampton, round 2**

Before foreign players became such a fashion accessory that every top British club had to have at least a dozen of them it was only a select few that ventured to these shores. With fond memories of Argentinians Ossie Ardiles and Ricky Villa at Spurs, Newcastle splashed out £575,000 on Brazilian centre-forward Mirandinha, reasoning that the new undersoil heating at St James' Park would help him acclimatize. He was bought to pacify fans mourning the sale of Peter Beardsley and Chris Waddle who were scared that their beloved Gazza would soon follow suit. Their worst fears were realized in the summer of 1988 when Paul Gascoigne joined Spurs for £2m. Big mistake: everyone knows that black and white stripes take pounds off you. Early next season he returned to Tyneside with his new team and was subjected to constant jeers of 'Fattie'. At least there was nothing wrong with the Newcastle fans' eyesight.

Meanwhile Mirandinha was suffering from enough ailments to warrant a special

A SPLINTER WAS LIABLE TO KEEP MIRANDINHA OUT FOR SIX WEEKS

☻ ODDBALL

WHEN GAZZA'S NEW TEAM SPURS VISITED NEWCASTLE ON THE SECOND SATURDAY OF THE 1988-89 SEASON, THE NEWCASTLE OLD BOY WAS BOMBARDED WITH MARS BARS.

edition of *The Lancet*. A splinter was liable to keep him out for six weeks while a nagging cold was deemed career threatening. When he did make it on to the pitch he appeared determined to do everything himself, thus proving to be the only Latin American male incapable of making a pass. In October the team's desperate form cost manager Willie McFaul his job. His successor, the experienced Jim Smith, soon consigned the costly Brazilian to the 'waste of money' bin where he joined Smith's bottle of anti-dandruff shampoo. When United were duly relegated after finishing bottom, Mirandinha knew his days were numbered. He had said he wanted to use the money he made in Newcastle to buy a pig farm outside Sao Paulo. A few of its inmates would need to fly before he was ever declared a local hero back on Tyneside.

Brazilian centre-forward Mirandinha: the only Latin American male incapable of making a pass.

CHARLTON ATHLETIC
1989-90

⊛ **League: 19th (Division 1)**
⊛ **FA Cup: 0-1 West Bromwich Albion, round 4**
⊛ **League Cup: 0-1 Southampton, round 3**

Between 1985 and 1992 a strange group of people wearing red and white anoraks could be seen roaming the streets of south and east London in search of a home. Without so much as a bundle of *Big Issues* to their name, they were small in number, often downcast but unfailingly polite. They were Charlton supporters. These shy nomads who, like the team they followed, tended to panic when a camera was pointed at them, came into being after

CHARLTON WERE THE CUCKOOS OF FOOTBALL

Charlton went into administration and were forced to move from The Valley. For the next seven years Charlton wandered the wilderness, sharing first with Crystal Palace at Selhurst Park and then with West Ham at Upton Park. They were the cuckoos of football. Clubs became wise to their tactics. Staff at other London grounds always ensured their gates were locked at night in case Charlton had moved in by the morning.

Season 1989-90 saw Charlton lodging at Selhurst Park. Although manager Lennie Lawrence had done a sterling job in such difficult circumstances, it was widely accepted that Charlton were no more likely to be seen challenging for honours than Jeremy Clarkson would appear in a floral pinafore and a pair of Marigolds. In a bid to preserve their tenuously held top-flight status, they signed defender Joe McLaughlin from Chelsea for £600,000 in pre-season but the real problems lay at the other end of the pitch where striker Paul Williams was woefully lacking in support. Which brings us to Carl Leaburn, the sort of cult hero who comes along maybe once in a lifetime. At 6ft 3in Leaburn should have been better in the air than easyJet but far from proving a real handful for defenders, his goals were as rare as an Alaskan heatwave. He had previously managed just three in fifty-two games and maintained the run by failing to score in his eight starts in 1989-90. But the crowd loved him … in the same way that owners love a three-legged greyhound. Leaburn's boundless enthusiasm

⚽ ODDBALL

WHEN CHARLTON BEAT WEST BROM IN FRONT OF THE CAMERAS ON 5 FEBRUARY 1995, IT WAS THEIR FIRST VICTORY ON LIVE TELEVISION SINCE THE 1947 FA CUP FINAL.

was matched only by his ineptitude. What with Robert Lee contributing one goal from thirty-seven appearances, Charlton struggled all season. As defeat followed defeat, heads began to drop faster than they did at the height of the French Revolution. With just thirty-one goals from thirty-eight games, Charlton finished second from bottom – and thirteen points from safety – despite notable victories over Chelsea and Manchester United.

However it was not all doom and gloom for Charlton that season. For a start, neighbours Millwall were the only team worse than them in the First Division. Also, stung by Greenwich Council's refusal to allow planning permission for the Valley, Charlton supporters decided to fight the council at the local elections in May 1990. There were rumours that Carl Leaburn was standing … since standing was very much his forte on the pitch. Even without him the Valley Party picked up 14,838 votes and managed to unseat the chairman of the planning committee! Two months later planning permission was finally granted for the derelict Valley and although Charlton didn't actually move back until the end of 1992, at least it gave them time to think about the colour scheme and whether to have the executive boxes facing the pitch.

Charlton striker Carl Leaburn was a cult hero for his enthusiastic failure to score, his goals were as rare as an Alaskan heatwave.

WEST HAM UNITED
1991-92

- **League: 22nd (Division 1)**
- **FA Cup: 2-3 Sunderland, round 5 replay**
- **League Cup: 1-2 Norwich City, round 4**

What West Ham really needed, as they struggled in the bottom three for most of the season, was Billy Bonds the player. Unfortunately they got Billy Bonds the manager. In midfield Bonds had been a fearless swash-buckling pirate, but in the managerial dugout that season he proved about as bold and effective as Captain Pugwash.

As it happened, it was in midfield that the Hammers' major problems lay. The chief creative attacking forces, Stuart Slater and Ian Bishop, played forty-one games apiece and contributed one goal between them. Joe Bugner would have packed more goalmouth punch. With Second Division Charlton sharing Upton Park for the season, a visiting Martian would have been hard pushed to tell which team was West Ham, which was Charlton and which was the Dagenham Girl Pipers. The Hammers' poor League form transferred itself to the FA Cup, where they needed two attempts to scrape past Conference team Farnborough despite both games being staged at Upton Park. As West Ham's crisis mirrored that of Walford Town's in *EastEnders*, word had it that Dot Cotton was thinking of applying for the job of Hammers'

DOT COTTON WAS THINKING OF APPLYING FOR THE JOB OF HAMMERS' MANAGER

manager, provided she could combine it with working at the launderette. Meanwhile West Ham continued to air their dirty washing in public and in February 200 fans staged a pitch protest against the club's bond scheme, although some turned up only because they had heard it was an anti-Bonds rally.

Whereas most clubs change their manager more often than Jim Royle changes his underpants, West Ham had always bucked that trend. Consequently Bonds remained in charge despite relegation and repaid the board's faith by taking the team straight back up. But in August 1994, with Bonds deciding he no longer needed the hassle, West Ham decided they no longer needed him. After twenty-seven years together it was the saddest parting since Bobby Charlton's combover.

⚽ ODDBALL

WEST HAM'S IAN WRIGHT WAS FINED AND BANNED FOR THREE MATCHES FOR TRASHING REFEREE ROB HARRIS'S ROOM AFTER BEING SENT OFF AGAINST LEEDS UNITED IN 1999.

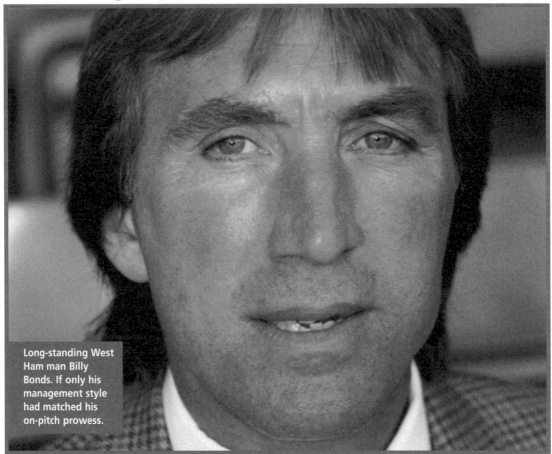

Long-standing West Ham man Billy Bonds. If only his management style had matched his on-pitch prowess.

England
1992 EUROPEAN CHAMPIONSHIPS FINALS

Ah, 1992, the Chinese year of the Turnip. After Graham Taylor was depicted by the *Sun* as a root vegetable following England's depressing exit from the European Championships, hunting him became a national pastime. Thankfully this entertainment has now been restricted and can be done by only two journalists at a time, meaning editors must call off a pack of newshounds. Furthermore they can follow only the scent of Taylor, not the man himself.

Many feel that the manager got a raw deal over the England job. It wasn't his fault that England had produced hardly any world-class players since 1966. Already deprived of Paul Gascoigne, John Barnes, Bryan Robson and Mark Wright, Taylor didn't have to dig much deeper to start scraping bottoms of barrels, caps being awarded to the likes of Keith Curle, Carlton Palmer, Andy Sinton and Tony Daley. The pool of talent barely came up to your ankles. Even the absent Lee Dixon was missed. Des Walker was a shadow of his former self and Gary Lineker had announced that he was retiring after the finals. Instead of Sinton and Daley he would be more concerned with cheese and onion.

If the qualifying performances were

GAMES SO BAD EVEN THE BALLBOYS WERE BOOED OFF

⚽ ODDBALL

UNOFFICIAL ENGLAND TEAM FAITH-HEALER EILEEN DREWERY CLAIMED THAT SHE PREVENTED IAN WRIGHT SCORING IN A 1997 WORLD CUP QUALIFIER IN ITALY (HE HIT THE POST IN THE LAST MINUTE) FOR FEAR THAT A GOAL MIGHT HAVE SPARKED CROWD TROUBLE.

lacklustre (seven goals from six games), England reserved their worst for the finals in Sweden. England were as drab and colourless as a November afternoon in Doncaster. Following goalless draws against Denmark and France (games so bad even the ballboys were booed off), England faced Sweden. David Platt raised false hopes early on but the hosts fought back and, after Taylor had controversially replaced Lineker in his last international with Arsenal's Alan Smith, Tomas Brolin sank England. Brolin would later put on enough weight to sink a small battleship. Taylor was roundly pilloried, not least for the perceived snub to Lineker that denied him the chance of equalling Bobby Charlton's England goalscoring record. It was like kicking away the Queen Mother's walking stick. Taylor's reputation never recovered but Dame Fortune had rarely smiled upon him. Meanwhile, England's success in the next major competition may depend on whether 2006 is the Chinese year of the Love Rat.

Housewives' favourite Gary Lineker: Euro '92 was his international swansong but England were more like ugly ducklings throughout the championships.

BIRMINGHAM CITY
1993-94

- ⚽ **League: 22nd (Division 1)**
- ⚽ **FA Cup: 1-2 Kidderminster Harriers, round 3**
- ⚽ **League Cup: 0-2 (aggregate) Aston Villa, round 2**

Barry Fry is one of those guys whom football supporters love … as long as he's not managing their club. A total enthusiast – and with the heart attacks to prove it – Fry breezes in and out of clubs like a chubby tornado, making headlines and leaving chaos and confusion in his wake. His friends say he's infectious … but so was the Black Death. Blessed with the poise and elegance of a dodgy second-hand car dealer, Fry has always enjoyed nothing more than

BARRY FRY IS INFECTIOUS … BUT SO WAS THE BLACK DEATH

dabbling in the transfer market. Constantly on the lookout for a bargain, he would sign a player, give him a few games – but then see an even better bargain on offer and sign him too. Consequently Birmingham, in common with Fry's other clubs, operated a revolving door policy where players would be shipped in and out frequently, barely staying long enough to acquire their own peg in the dressing room.

Fry arrived at St Andrew's in place of Terry Cooper in December 1993. The team were already struggling in soccer's second tier but the bullish Bazza reckoned he could turn things around if he was allowed to bring in a few players. By the end of the season

⚽ ODDBALL

WHEN HE WAS MANAGER OF BARNET, BARRY FRY WAS ONCE SEEN MOWING THE UNDERHILL PITCH BY MOONLIGHT AT FOUR O'CLOCK IN THE MORNING. HE TOLD INVESTIGATING POLICE OFFICERS THAT HE WAS SO WORKED UP ABOUT THAT AFTERNOON'S MATCH THAT HE COULDN'T SLEEP AND HAD DECIDED TO DO SOMETHING USEFUL INSTEAD.

Birmingham had used a staggering forty players in their unsuccessful fight against the drop with only one – striker Andy Saville – making more than thirty appearances. By contrast champions Crystal Palace used only twenty-two in the course of the season. Birmingham players often met their teammates for the first time on match days – sometimes, one suspected, while the coin was being tossed. It was more like speed dating than football management.

In Fry's first month at the club alone he spent £1.27 million on nine new players, but failed to find a drawing, let alone a winning, formula. Then Birmingham were paired with neighbours Kidderminster Harriers of the Conference in the third round of the FA Cup. Although Kidderminster had never beaten a League club in their 108-year history, Fry feared the worst and, sure enough, the visitors – aided by a Saville penalty miss – pulled off the shock of the round. Fry was beside himself although with his girth, it was sometimes an optical illusion. At the final reckoning Birmingham were relegated on goal difference beneath local rivals West Brom. And Fry was probably still telling the board that a couple more new signings would have made all the difference …

Birmingham City manager Barry Fry – a football legend, but for all the wrong reasons.

ARSENAL

1994-95

- **League: 12th (Premiership)**
- **FA Cup: 0-2 Millwall, round 3 replay**
- **League Cup: 0-1 Liverpool, round 5**
- **European Cup-Winners' Cup: 1-2 Real Zaragoza, final**

The Highbury faithful were taking bets on which would happen first: the colonization of Mars, Lord Lucan presenting *Wish You Were Here?* or a John Jensen goal for Arsenal. The Danish midfielder had gone ninety-seven scoreless games for the Gunners until, on the last day of 1994, he finally broke his duck during the 3-1 home defeat by Queens Park Rangers. News of Jensen's goal sent shock waves

NOTHING BECKONED BEYOND MID-TABLE MEDIOCRITY

through the world. The immediate impact was that Arsenal lost to Spurs at White Hart Lane before being dumped out of the Cup by First Division Millwall, and Robbie Williams left Take That.

Jensen's joy was about the only bright spot in a miserable season for Arsenal. Paul Merson confessed to drink, drug and gambling problems. (What's the difference between Paul Merson and a can of Coca-Cola? – One's red and white and full of coke, the other's a soft drinks container.) And manager George Graham was sacked over financial irregularities after opening more envelopes than you see on Oscars night. His assistant, Stewart Houston, took over the

⚽ ODDBALL

AFTER SCORING THE WINNER IN THE 1993 COCA-COLA CUP FINAL YOUNG ARSENAL MIDFIELDER STEVE MORROW BROKE HIS ARM WHEN, IN THE POST-MATCH CELEBRATIONS, SKIPPER TONY ADAMS PUT HIM OVER HIS SHOULDER AND ACCIDENTALLY DROPPED HIM.

reins and promptly steered Arsenal to a first home win in four months, but nothing beckoned beyond mid-table mediocrity. Even the rock of the team's previous success – the synchronized offside back four of Lee Dixon, Steve Bould, Tony Adams and Nigel Winterburn – was starting to show cracks. And when Andy Linighan was forced to step in, it was noticeable that he was always

Goalie David Seaman watches as yet another ball sails past him into the net. It was a sight much seen all season.

that split second behind the other three when raising his hand to appeal. He just hadn't mastered the routine. It was much the same when Jenny first replaced Kerry in Atomic Kitten.

Yet against all the odds there was hope of a trophy when Arsenal travelled to Paris for the European Cup-Winners' Cup final against Spain's Real Zaragoza. However, in the last minute of extra-time with the score at 1-1, Nayim – a former Spurs player to boot – lobbed David Seaman from 50 yards. The goalkeeper flapped and back-pedalled in vain. Somewhere in the stand a Mr Ronaldinho was taking notes …

IPSWICH TOWN

1994-95

- ⚽ **League: 22nd (Premiership)**
- ⚽ **FA Cup: 1-2 Wrexham, round 3**
- ⚽ **League Cup: 0-4 Bolton (aggregate), round 2**

With most local derbies you can understand the animosity. Rangers versus Celtic represents bigoted, sectarian hatred; Southampton and Portsmouth stems from Navy rivalry; in Liverpool, Manchester, Sheffield, Bristol etc. it is about divisions and loyalties within the city. But Ipswich and Norwich, what's that all about? Neither place could be termed a soccer hotbed. 'Canaries'? It's not quite in the same league as 'Lions', 'Tigers' or even 'Seagulls'.

JEFFREY ARCHER HAD A BETTER DEFENCE THAN IPSWICH

What's the worst thing a canary can do to you? Sing out of tune? And, when your chief cheerleader is a middle-England TV cook, we're not exactly talking tribal warfare. So, to the outsider at least, this simmering feud seems nothing more than a spat between two old farmers as to who has the better marrow at the local vegetable show.

The 1994-95 season saw both teams relegated from the Premiership but Norwich City held local bragging rights, not only by finishing two places above Ipswich but also by completing the double over them. Norwich were not exactly unique in that respect, since Jeffrey Archer had a better defence than Ipswich. They conceded a staggering ninety-three goals – more than two a game – to make goalkeeper Craig Forrest the busiest man in East Anglia (apart from the owner of the local inbreeding farm). With things looking blacker than a Goth wedding, manager John Lyall received the traditional pre-Christmas sack from Santa and was replaced by George Burley. Defeat in the Cup to Second Division Wrexham was followed by a run of eight straight defeats, including a 9-0 mauling at Old Trafford. Ian Marshall, who always looked like the lost member of Spinal Tap, managed a couple of goals late in the season but Ipswich's fate had long been sealed. Hostilities would be renewed in Division One with basted turkeys at dawn.

⚽ ODDBALL

WHEN IPSWICH MANAGER JOE ROYLE BECAME BOSS OF OLDHAM ATHLETIC IN 1982, HE ARRIVED FOR HIS FIRST DAY AT WORK IN THE CAB OF A COAL LORRY. HE HAD BEEN FORCED TO HITCH A LIFT AFTER HIS CAR BROKE DOWN ON THE WAY TO BOUNDARY PARK.

Ipswich vs Norwich – as fierce as it gets in East Anglia, as Jon Newsome (left) and Ian Marshall battle it out for the ball.

SOUTHAMPTON
1995-96

- **League: 17th (Premiership)**
- **FA Cup: 2-6 Tottenham Hotspur, round 5 replay**
- **League Cup: 1-2 Reading, round 4**

When Alan Ball left Southampton to become Manchester City's problem, Dave Merrington, coach at The Dell for eleven years, was elevated to manager. As for Stevie Wonder on a ladder, the step up is notoriously difficult and, while Ball may not have cast the longest of shadows, even he proved a tough act for Merrington to follow.

As usual the team's hopes rested firmly on the shoulders of Matt Le Tissier, viewed by Saints fans as the best news to come out of the Channel Islands since Mike and Bernie Winters announced they were no longer doing summer seasons. Le Tissier was supremely gifted. When God dealt out the talent among footballers, you didn't have to look far to see who got Carlton Palmer's share. Only a leper could drop a shoulder like Le Tissier. But the great man managed only seven League goals in 1995-96 (three of them penalties), as a result of which Saints hovered dangerously above the relegation places. Ultimately it needed a goalless draw at home to Wimbledon in the final game of the season to secure Southampton's safety on goal difference ahead of … Manchester City. It was good to

SAINTS HOVERED DANGEROUSLY ABOVE THE RELEGATION PLACES

Not even the talents of Matt Le Tissier could help Southampton this season … particularly when he insisted on playing 'piggy in the middle' with the Magpies.

⚽ ODDBALL

AFTER BREAKING HIS ARM IN A MATCH AT LEICESTER IN 1998-99 SOUTHAMPTON DEFENDER FRANCIS BENALI REPEATED THE FEAT A MONTH LATER WHILE SWEEPING UP LEAVES IN HIS GARDEN.

know that Ball hadn't lost his touch. Yet the most eventful game of the season was a 6-2 home defeat by Spurs in the Cup, courtesy of a Ronny Rosenthal hat-trick – a remarkable feat in itself as Devon Loch was a better finisher than Rosenthal.

Although Merrington had kept the team up, he was not invited to stay on as manager. But in one respect, he fared better than his many successors at Southampton. After all, what could be worse than being sacked by a bloke called Rupert?

BOLTON WANDERERS
1995-96

- ⚽ **League: 20th (Premiership)**
- ⚽ **FA Cup: 0-1 Leeds United, round 4**
- ⚽ **League Cup: 2-3 (on penalties) Norwich City, round 4 replay**

As with all businesses football goes through certain vogues. There have been crazes for plastic pitches, the diamond formation, signing American internationals just because they've got over a hundred caps. Even Sven was once all the rage. Similarly there was a time when joint managers were in fashion. It all started with Alan Curbishley and Steve Gritt at Charlton and, when that proved a short-term success,

BOLTON WERE LIKE WORZEL GUMMIDGE – A SHAMBOLIC OUTFIT

others followed suit, usually with calamitous consequences. For just as two heads are better than one, too many cooks spoil the broth. A case in point was the partnership of former Derby and England teammates Roy McFarland and Colin Todd at Bolton Wanderers in 1995. What they lacked in managerial experience at the highest level they made up for with immaculate grooming. Todd, in particular, could have modelled blazers in a Littlewoods catalogue. He would no more be seen sporting a mullet than Sam Allardyce would be seen with a ponytail or Christian Gross would be seen with a manager-of-the-month award.

⚽ ODDBALL

IN MAY 2003 REVEREND ROGER OLDFIELD, A BOLTON SUPPORTER FOR THIRTY YEARS, HELD A SPECIAL SERVICE, OFFERING PRAYERS FOR THE CLUB TO AVOID RELEGATION. ALL ATTENDEES WERE GIVEN ORANGES HALFWAY THROUGH THE SERVICE WHILE A SAM ALLARDYCE LOOKALIKE FROM THE CONGREGATION BARKED ORDERS FROM A MAKESHIFT DUGOUT AT THE FRONT OF THE CHURCH.

Alas, Bolton, on their return to the top flight, were more like Worzel Gummidge – a shambolic outfit whose victory over Wimbledon on 13 January was only their third win of the season. Although the management team had paid a club record £1.5m for Barnsley defender Gerry Taggart, it was a lack of goals that sounded Bolton's death knell. The strike force of John McGinlay, Fabian De Freitas and Nathan Blake carried all the menace of a Tim Henman snarl. With Wanderers eight points adrift at the bottom, McFarland was relieved of his duties in January, allowing Todd to take sole charge. Around that time Tony Blair was promising 'Things can only get better'. He had obviously not been to Bolton. For Wanderers finished bottom of the Premiership, having lost twenty-five of their thirty-eight games. Even so, theirs wasn't the worst record that year. Gina G saw to that.

Bolton clash with Leeds in the FA Cup fourth round.

FULHAM
1995-96

⚽ **League: 18th (Division 3)**
⚽ **FA Cup: 1-2 Shrewsbury, round 3 replay**
⚽ **League Cup: 1-7 (aggregate)**
   Wolverhampton Wanderers, round 2

Before the Harrods van parked outside the main entrance of Craven Cottage, Fulham were everyone's favourite aunt: delightfully dotty, always a welcome visitor and never likely to give you a beating. But years of neglect and the onset of Alzheimer's – she couldn't remember when she'd last won a trophy – had left the old girl at serious risk of being sectioned in the Conference. The man charged with keeping away the men in white coats was Ian Branfoot, who had previously been hounded out of Southampton. Indeed he could not have been more reviled by fans at The Dell had he been waving a Portsmouth season ticket.

Bringing all the tact of Trinny and Susannah to Craven Cottage, Branfoot set about matters in a typically no-nonsense fashion. He overhauled the playing staff, bringing in so many ageing players that Saga thought about becoming the shirt sponsor. It did not go unnoticed that a number of the recruits had a spell with Southampton on their CV. He favoured direct football, destined, it seemed, to take Fulham directly to the bottom of the table.

SAGA THOUGHT ABOUT BECOMING THE SHIRT SPONSOR

Manager Ian Branfoot confidently displays an armpit free from sweat patch. He may have kept his cool; his job was another matter.

Without a win for twelve games, Branfoot was rapidly becoming as unpopular as he had been at Southampton – except that Fulham fans were generally too polite to resort to abusive threats. When it came to radical revolution they favoured the Sergeant Wilson approach.

With the team's fortunes at their lowest ebb, they somehow conjured up a 7-0 hammering of Second Division Swansea in the first round of the FA Cup. The result came as such a shock that the obituaries column in the following week's *Fulham & Hammersmith Chronicle* was double its normal length. The expected improvement in form didn't follow, however, and in February 1996 Branfoot stepped aside to allow player-coach Micky Adams to become the League's youngest boss.

Adams steadied the ship to preserve League status and went on to lead Fulham

⚽ ODDBALL

SENEGAL MIDFIELDER PAPA BOUBA DIOP REPORTEDLY PERFORMED A VOODOO CEREMONY INVOLVING THE SPRINKLING OF ANIMAL BLOOD AROUND THE CRAVEN COTTAGE PITCH IN AN ATTEMPT TO PUT THE MAGIC BACK INTO FULHAM'S 2004-05 SEASON.

to promotion in 1997. But when his Harrods hamper arrived, it contained his P45. And not even a Scotch egg.

EVERTON
1997-98

- **League: 17th (Premiership)**
- **FA Cup: 0-1 Newcastle, round 3**
- **League Cup: 1-4 Coventry, round 3**

There are four great mysteries in life. Why did God give men nipples? How does the guy who drives the snowplough get to work? Why do people eat cooked breakfasts off the open pages of library books? And how have Everton managed to stay in the top division for over fifty years?

For too many seasons, particularly in the 1990s, the Toffeemen cheated the drop at the last minute, invariably owing their survival to one man – Welsh goalkeeper Neville Southall. But by 1997 the former dustman, whose general demeanour suggested he still rummaged in bins on his days off, was nearing the end of his Everton career. Manager Howard Kendall was back for an unprecedented third term, something that the American constitution has wisely ensured will be denied to George W. Bush. Kendall relied on the little and large strike force of Nick Barmby and Duncan Ferguson but there were times when Syd and Eddie themselves would not have looked out of place in the Everton attack. Ferguson, for all his physical threat, has never been a prolific goalscorer while Barmby must be the only person in Britain to be homesick for Hull.

EVERTON WERE JUST LIKE THE TITANIC

Everton stalwart Duncan Ferguson dramatically uproots Newcastle's Alessandro Pistone.

This was to prove an especially traumatic season for Evertonians, a Gary Speed penalty against Leicester just before Christmas ending a run of eight games without a win. At least there would be something to celebrate that Christmas – and to compensate for the Sonia CD in their stocking.

While fans vented their anger at chairman Peter Johnson rather than Kendall, the team succeeded where Robert Maxwell had failed by just about keeping their heads above water. It all boiled down to the final game – at home to Coventry. Although Barmby missed a penalty, a 1-1 draw was enough to keep Everton up on goal difference, thanks to Chelsea's victory over Bolton. Before the kick-off against Coventry, Everton women's team took a bow for winning their league and the club's youth team were applauded for winning the FA Youth Cup. As one wag remarked, Everton were just like the *Titanic* – women and children first. He did not need to add … and sinking fast.

⚽ ODDBALL

DESPERATE FOR A TRANSFER, EVERTON KEEPER NEVILLE SOUTHALL STAGED A HALF-TIME PROTEST DURING A 1990 MATCH WITH LEEDS. WHILE HIS TEAMMATES WERE IN THE DRESSING ROOM, A MOROSE SOUTHALL SAT ALONE ON THE PITCH AT THE FOOT OF A GOALPOST.

MANCHESTER CITY
1997-98

- ⚽ **League: 22nd (Division 1)**
- ⚽ **FA Cup: 1-2 West Ham, round 4**
- ⚽ **League Cup: 2-4 (on penalties) Blackpool, round 1**

You only have to look at some celebrities to tell which team they support. Actor Alan Davies appears calm and laid-back because he supports Arsenal; Jo Brand needs a great sense of humour because she follows Crystal Palace; Angus Deayton has an air of superiority because he supports Manchester United; and the Gallagher brothers are psychotic because they support Manchester City. Ever since the days of Joe Mercer and Malcolm Allison, following City

ONLY CITY COULD SCORE FIVE AND GO DOWN

has been more of a ghost train than a rollercoaster simply because you never know what's lurking round the corner. At their best, to paraphrase Swiss Toni, watching City was like making love to a beautiful woman – exciting, breathtaking and dangerous; at their worst it was like making love to an old slapper – painful, unhealthy and best done with your eyes shut. The best bit was the break when you changed ends.

The 1997-98 season saw City playing in the second tier. Their manager was Frank Clark, a man with the permanent expression of a benevolent bloodhound. His dour voice gave the impression that he was better suited to making station announcements at Manchester Piccadilly than delivering rousing Churchillian speeches at half-time. With City facing relegation to the third grade for the first time in their 111-year history, Clark was replaced in February by the admirable Joe Royle. Some people say Royle has a chip on his shoulder, others say that's because he's got a potato for a head. But, despite signing assorted Russians and Georgians whose main functions were to keep their one star player, Georgi Kinkladze, company and to use up the tricky consonants in Soccer Scrabble, City were relegated. Typically inconsistent, they won their final game 5-2 at Stoke, sending both teams down. Their fans were left to reflect that only Manchester City could score five and go down.

Uwe Rösler: not initiating an upbeat team display of 'Heads, Shoulders, Knees and Toes', but showing his dejection after missing a penalty.

⚽ ODDBALL

IN MARCH 1999 A DISENCHANTED MANCHESTER CITY FAN THREW AN ASTHMA INHALER ON TO THE MAINE ROAD PITCH DURING A FEEBLE DRAW WITH NORTHAMPTON TOWN.

NOTTINGHAM FOREST
1998-99

- ⚽ **League: 20th (Premiership)**
- ⚽ **FA Cup: 0-1 Portsmouth, round 3**
- ⚽ **League Cup: 1-2 Manchester United, round 4**

Whereas Brian Clough succeeded in making a silk purse out of a sow's ear, his successors barely mustered a packet of bacon crisps between them. Their cause was not helped by the unrealistic expectations of Forest fans, who thought their club still had a divine right to be in Europe with a team that was often barely the best in Nottingham. By 1998 Forest's only hope of getting into Europe was to sign Judith Chalmers.

The season was doomed before it started

A CLUTCH OF CUT-PRICE FOREIGN IMPORTS

with Forest's star player, petulant Dutch striker Pierre van Hooijdonk, refusing to train with the club because he thought his teammates weren't good enough for the Premiership. He may have been a pain, but he was a shrewd judge of ability. While he went on strike, the rest of the team played as if they had come out in sympathy. Although van Hooijdonk did eventually play a few games, his piqued teammates refused to hug or kiss him when he scored. Definitely no tongues. Fielding a clutch of cut-price foreign imports such as Jean-Claude Darcheville, Jesper Mattsson, Hugo Porfirio and Stale Stensaas, Forest continued to struggle and

Pierre van Hooijdonk (airborne) was about as popular among Forest players as a mumps epidemic.

beleaguered boss Dave Bassett was sacked in January.

Ron Atkinson was put in charge until the end of the season and marked his first home game by going to the wrong dugout. Further proof that he had lost his way came when he paid £1.1m to make Carlton Palmer his first signing. The highlight of Big Ron's reign was an 8-1 home defeat by Manchester United, which he described tongue-in-cheek as 'a nine-goal thriller'. When Forest finished bottom of the table, he announced his retirement from management to concentrate on what used to be called his media career. The board reacted by naming David Platt as the new manager. The Forest faithful will always be grateful to Platt. For without him they would never have had the chance to witness the three hapless Italians – Salvatore Matrecano, Moreno Mannini and Gianluca Petrachi. Their signings rekindled memories of a previous Forest Italian import, Andrea Silenzi, a man described as an old-fashioned centre-forward. And in truth he was almost as good as Nat Lofthouse. But then Nat Lofthouse is eighty.

⚽ ODDBALL

AFTER HIS OWN-GOAL HAD SEEN NOTTINGHAM FOREST PROMOTED TO DIVISION ONE IN 1977, MILLWALL'S JON MOORE WAS VOTED PLAYER OF THE YEAR BY GRATEFUL FOREST SUPPORTERS.

GLASGOW CELTIC
1999-2000

- ⚬ **League: 2nd (Scottish Premier)**
- ⚬ **Scottish FA Cup: 1-3 Inverness Caledonian Thistle, round 3**
- ⚬ **Scottish League Cup: Winners**
- ⚬ **UEFA Cup: 0-2 (aggregate) Olympique Lyon, round 2**

With Celtic in ailing health, it was decided that the team required urgent medical attention. Of course the club could have brought in Alan Ball to perform the last rites but instead they hoped that Czech coach Dr Jozef Venglos might be able to come up with a cure … despite the fact that he had previously failed to bring about any discernible improvement in the condition of Aston Villa. In his sole year in charge at Celtic Park, Rangers won the treble. Dr Jo became Dr No. Celtic gently eased him aside in the summer of 1999 and in his place unveiled what they hoped would become their Dream Team – the personable, media-friendly John Barnes in his first managerial post, with the taciturn but vastly experienced Kenny Dalglish as technical director of football.

THE TEAM REQUIRED URGENT MEDICAL ATTENTION

Go into a football club and anyone can instantly tell you what the kit man does, what the secretary does and so on. Yet nobody has the faintest idea what a well-paid technical director does, often least of all the man himself. The post is soccer's

'Technical director' Kenny Dalglish. You'd have that glint in your eye and the dimple in your cheek if you had his job – and his salary.

version of the consultant. Many cynics expressed their own ideas about Dalglish's interpretation of the role, usually involving the perfection of his golf game.

It was clear from the outset that Barnes was in sole charge of team affairs – but he was an eager Boy Scout trying to run a multinational company. The job, as it was for Gareth Gates with Jordan, was simply too big for him. Quite apart from the traditional early exit in Europe, results were disappointing, coming to a head in February with a humiliating home defeat in the Cup to little Inverness Caledonian Thistle – a result that prompted the classic headline: SUPER CALEY GO BALLISTIC – CELTIC ARE ATROCIOUS. With Dalglish taking over as Mary Poppins until the end of the season, Barnes was hastily ushered out of the door, his chief legacy to football thus remaining the 'Anfield Rap'.

⚽ ODDBALL

CELTIC FANS WHO SAT DOWN TO WATCH TV HIGHLIGHTS OF THEIR TEAM'S 7-1 THRASHING OF RANGERS IN THE 1957 SCOTTISH LEAGUE CUP FINAL WERE ABLE TO SEE ONLY THE FIRST HALF – BECAUSE THE CAMERAMAN HAD FORGOTTEN TO REMOVE THE LENS CAP AFTER THE HALF-TIME BREAK.

Germany
2000 EUROPEAN CHAMPIONSHIPS FINALS

There wasn't much for Kevin Keegan's England to smile about at Euro 2000. It was the usual story of being outplayed by countries that weren't fit to lace the drinks fifty years ago. But in the depths of despair at another early exit, there was one unlikely consolation: the Germans were even worse. Everyone admires German efficiency – except in the sporting arena. Quite simply, they are too good at too many sports and don't seem to have grasped the British concept of heroic failure. Losing is as alien to a German as foreplay is to an Australian. Cliff Richard was still a young one and Gerry didn't need a pacemaker the last time England had beaten the Germans in a meaningful encounter, so the chance to settle old scores was eagerly anticipated.

THE GERMANS REALLY WERE CRAP

Going into Euro 2000, the word on the streets was that the Germans were nothing exceptional. The appointment of coach Erich Ribbeck had been criticized because he was never an international player, and striker Oliver Bierhoff – hero of Euro '96 – had openly questioned his squad selection. But we had heard it all before. How many times had we been told that the Germans

⊗ ODDBALL

APPROPRIATELY NAMED GERMAN MIDFIELDER STEFAN EFFENBERG WAS SENT HOME FROM THE 1994 WORLD CUP FINALS AFTER GIVING GERMAN FANS THE FINGER DURING HIS COUNTRY'S UNCONVINCING VICTORY OVER SOUTH KOREA.

weren't as good as usual, only for them to be battling through to the latter stages of a tournament long after our pampered Premiership stars had landed back at Heathrow? But this time was different: the Germans really were crap. Combative goalkeeper Oliver Kahn, who always looked likely to undergo a dramatic transformation

Lothar Matthäus was running in only one direction: home.

when there was a full moon, was constantly complaining about a lack of protection. If only his mother had voiced similar thoughts … In the middle, Lothar Matthäus tried valiantly to defy the march of time but any attack that relied heavily on the lumbering Carsten Jancker was destined to struggle. Jancker – Germany's answer to Emile Heskey – is said to have been looking for a move to a London club, presumably unaware that he is already part of Cockney rhyming slang.

After drawing with Romania in their opening group game, Germany succumbed to an Alan Shearer goal in the one that mattered. Portugal, having already qualified, then fielded nine reserves but still humbled the Germans 3-0. The highlight was the second goal, Kahn allowing a soft shot from Sergio Conceição to slip under his body. The laughter could be heard all the way back to Jens Lehmann's house. Germany finished bottom of the group, the first time for sixteen years that they had failed to progress beyond the first stage. Now they knew what the rest of us had to put up with.

MIDDLESBROUGH

2000-01

- ☻ **League: 14th (Premiership)**
- ☻ **FA Cup: 1-3 Wimbledon, round 4 replay**
- ☻ **League Cup: 0-1 Wimbledon, round 3**

To some clubs a massive cash injection means being able to paint the crush barriers. To Middlesbrough in the 1990s, chairman Steve Gibson's millions transformed the club from near bankruptcy to a position where they could afford to sign the best players in the world. The man entrusted with spending Gibson's cash wisely was Bryan Robson. Some think Gibson would have earned a better return for his money by investing in Betamax. Over a six-year period Robson attracted star names to Teesside, many labouring under the misapprehension that Redcar beach was the next best thing to the Copacabana. Once they got a whiff of their new surroundings, some got straight on to their agent … and then their travel agent. So the brochure was changed to call the new ground the Riverside Stadium, but attempts to portray it as a *Wind in the Willows* setting proved equally unsuccessful. 'Ratty and Mole Visit the Chemical Works' was never high on Kenneth Grahame's agenda.

IT WAS LIKE WATCHING ASTROTURF GROW

With little continuity, the limit of Robson's ambition seemed to be to avoid a second relegation. He answered his critics by pointing out that he had put

Middlesbrough on the map. And Jack the Ripper put Whitechapel on the map.

For the 2000-01 season Robson had assembled another expensive squad, including Ugo Ehiogu, Paul Ince and Alen Boksic. By winter results were so bad that Robson wore the haunted look of a politician on *Newsnight* who has just been told that Kirsty Wark is on holiday. With the fans on Robson's back, Gibson sent for Terry Venables to help out the under-fire manager.

⚽ ODDBALL

A TEENAGE MIDDLESBROUGH FAN TRIED TO GET ROUND A COURT CURFEW BY WEARING A GORILLA SUIT TO A 1992 LEAGUE CUP TIE AGAINST PETERBOROUGH. BUT WHEN HIS TEAM SCORED, HE THREW THE HEAD INTO THE AIR IN CELEBRATION AND WAS LATER SPOTTED BY A VIGILANT POLICE OFFICER WHO WAS WATCHING THE HIGHLIGHTS ON TV.

Calling in Venables to solve a crisis is a bit like pouring water on a chip-pan fire, but it is an indication of how desperate things were that even he couldn't fail to bring about a marked improvement. By organizing things at the back he made Middlesbrough hard to beat … and even harder to watch. It was like watching Astroturf grow.

In the end, fourteenth place was a decent finish for Middlesbrough fans. And there was better news on the way: Gibson was looking for a new manager.

Alen Boksic: at least Robson's expensive Boro rose above Bradford City. On this occasion.

LEICESTER CITY

2001-02

- **League: 20th (Premiership)**
- **FA Cup: 0-1 West Brom, round 4**
- **League Cup: 0-6 Leeds United, round 3**

As any football supporter will confirm, the close season is usually a time for unwarranted optimism. No matter how badly your team played the previous season or how dismal your new signings (if any), once the fixtures come out at the end of June reality gives way to dreams. Even East Stirling fans can picture picking up the odd draw before the end of November. But when you lose your first game of the season 5-0 at home to Bolton, the omens are so bad that Mr Micawber would have struggled to put on a brave face. This was the grim scenario that faced Leicester supporters in August 2001 – and just to prove that the Bolton result was no fluke, City crashed 4-0 at Highbury in their next game. Manager Peter Taylor was already under fire for spending £25 million on a string of signings that were an even bigger mystery than Owen Hargreaves's twenty-six England caps. The regular fall guy was £5 million striker Ade Akinbiyi who looked about as comfortable in the Premiership as Roy Cropper at the wheel of a McLaren. After those opening two hammerings goalkeeper Tim Flowers lost his place to Ian Walker, but soon Taylor

A GRIM SCENARIO FACED LEICESTER SUPPORTERS

⚽ ODDBALL

TWO LEICESTER PLAYERS – STAN MILBURN AND JACK FROGGATT – COMBINED TO PRODUCE SOCCER'S ONLY INSTANCE OF A SHARED OWN-GOAL. PLAYING AGAINST CHELSEA IN DECEMBER 1954, THE PAIR LUNGED AT THE BALL IN AN ATTEMPT TO CLEAR AND CONNECTED SIMULTANEOUSLY TO SEND IT FLYING INTO THEIR OWN NET.

needed snookers and it came as no surprise when he was relieved of his duties a little over a month into the season – with Leicester planted at the foot of the table and sending out roots.

Dave Bassett took over and moulded Taylor's team in his own image – experienced, competitive, but limited. With Robbie Savage, Dennis Wise and Frank Sinclair, the side packed a bite that a piranha would have been proud of but only Muzzy Izzet exuded class. Leicester were bottom on Boxing Day and, in a world of few certainties, just about the surest was that they would stay there for the rest of the season. By the end Akinbiyi weighed in with just two goals from sixteen starts, leaving veteran Brian Deane as top scorer with six. In April, just before relegation was confirmed, Bassett was moved upstairs to become director of football, his number two, Micky Adams, taking over as manager to plot the return journey. And so Leicester's last season at Filbert Street, their home since 1891, ended in despair, despite the players managing to rouse themselves for the final game at the old ground, beating Spurs 2-1 to record only their fifth Premiership victory of the campaign. Nevertheless, that summer City fans were confident of bouncing straight back. And for once they were right – although the team has continued to go up and down like a whore's drawers.

Class apart: Muzzy Izzet, a rose among thorns, yet none of those with points enough to save the team from relegation.

France
2002 WORLD CUP FINALS

National supporters react in different ways to exits from major soccer tournaments. In England the mentally challenged choose to riot in small provincial towns that are hotbeds of bowls rather than football; in Italy they throw insults and tomatoes at the players; and in France they simply shrug their shoulders and return to their wine. As the reigning world and European champions France were hot favourites in South Korea and Japan but a stuttering warm-up campaign indicated that maybe all was not well with Roger Lemerre's men. Suddenly their famous 'va va voom' was beginning to sound more like the engine of a Skoda being

ZIDANE WAS WHEELED OUT BUT HE WAS A PALE IMITATION OF HIS NORMAL SELF

started on a frosty morning. Robert Pires was already ruled out with injury and, worse still, the world's most accomplished footballer, Zinedine Zidane, injured his left thigh in the warm-up match with South Korea, as a result of which he missed the first two games of the finals. Nevertheless Lemerre was still able to call on world-class performers … and Frank Leboeuf.

The opening match saw France pitted against unfancied Senegal, who were making their first appearance in the finals. Beforehand, the Africans pinpointed Leboeuf as France's weakest link and so it proved as his ageing legs struggled to keep pace with the speedy Senegalese forwards. It was like watching Dixon of Dock Green chasing two teenage muggers. And when a mix-up between Emmanuel Petit and the ever eccentric Fabien Barthez gifted Papa Bouba Diop the only goal of the game, Senegal had pulled off the biggest shock in world football since Steve McManaman was seen breaking into a sweat. The only good news for the French was that Leboeuf had joined the injury list.

Their next opponents were Uruguay but the game ended in a disappointing goalless draw, France suffering a further blow when Thierry Henry was sent off in the first half for a bad tackle. It was his only contribution to the tournament. Without Henry France now needed to beat Denmark in their final group game. Zidane was wheeled out, his left thigh heavily strapped, but he was a pale imitation of his normal self and the Danes won 2-0. John Motson probably told us that it was

⚽ ODDBALL

AT THE START OF A FRENCH CLUB MATCH IN 1950 ONE OF THE CAPTAINS ACCIDENTALLY SWALLOWED THE FIVE-FRANC PIECE WHICH THE REFEREE WAS TOSSING FOR CHOICE OF ENDS.

the first time France had lost a competitive fixture with Zidane in the side since he made his international debut in 1994. France thus became the first reigning champions to be knocked out at the opening stage of a World Cup tournament since Brazil in 1966. Before Lemerre's inevitable sacking the French camp said there were no excuses for their lamentable displays … apart from injuries, bad luck – and unsatisfactory croissants at the team hotel. Sent home without a win or even a goal to their name, the players might have expected a rough ride on their return to Paris. But on the Champs Elysées fans simply gave a familiar Gallic shrug.

Early exit: Zinedine Zidane holds his head, France no longer hold the World Cup.

ASTON VILLA
2002-03

- **League: 16th (Premiership)**
- **FA Cup: 1-4 Blackburn, round 3**
- **League Cup: 3-4 Liverpool, round 5**

It was on 16 September 2002 that Villa fans knew this would be a season to forget. That Monday evening, during a fiercely contested Birmingham derby at St Andrew's, Villa's Finnish goalkeeper Peter Enckelman allowed an Olof Mellberg throw-in to squirm under his foot and into the net. It was a blunder that would have made Abi Titmuss blush. Birmingham went on to complete the double over their great rivals, ensuring that Villa fans had even less to cheer about than usual. For, if Chelsea,

VILLA ARE DULLER THAN A NIGEL MANSELL VICTORY SPEECH

Arsenal and Manchester United are the stylish designer suits of the Premiership, Villa are the beige cardigan. They rarely stray far from mid-table, with the result that their season usually starts to wind down the day after the third round of the FA Cup. And a goal is such a rarity that it is greeted with the same hysteria accorded an English name on the Arsenal team-sheet. Quite simply, Villa are duller than a Nigel Mansell victory speech.

Chairman Doug Ellis – only Rome hasn't been sacked by Deadly Doug – is renowned for keeping a tight grip on the purse strings. Captain Hook is the only person to have put his hands in his pockets less. The club's transfer kitty still

⚽ ODDBALL

VILLA STRIKER SAVO MILOSEVIC WAS TRANSFER-LISTED IN 1998 AFTER SPITTING AT HIS OWN FANS DURING A DEFEAT AT BLACKBURN.

contains pound notes. Indeed, critics say that prising transfer funds from Ellis is football's equivalent of a Mick Jagger paternity suit – like getting blood out of a Stone. Given this perceived lack of ambition – Doug calls it 'prudent housekeeping' – Villa have sometimes struggled to attract top managers. But even the fans were shocked in 2002 when Graham Taylor swapped his role on the board for a second stint in charge.

Taylor has always had a fondness for beanpole strikers. In his first spell he utilized Ian Ormondroyd, who was more of a danger to planes taking off from Birmingham International Airport than he was to the opposition goal. This time Taylor gave the lanky Peter Crouch fourteen games. He proved equally effective, failing to hit the target once. There *were* good strikers at Villa Park, but mostly in visiting teams. In the Cup old boy Dwight Yorke scored twice for Blackburn to silence the Holte End, not that it needed much that season. By January Villa had scored just four goals in ten away League games before pulling off a 5-2 win at Middlesbrough. Normal service was quickly resumed, however. At the back Villa were reasonably solid. Steve Staunton was like a steamroller – with acceleration to match – and, although they flirted with relegation, it never reached the heavy petting stage. That would have been too much like excitement.

Look back in anguish: Aston Villa's Enckelman takes in the horror of his gaffe against Birmingham City and puts his head in his hands. It's a wonder he didn't drop it.

LIVERPOOL
2002-03

- ☻ **League: 5th (Premiership)**
- ☻ **FA Cup: 0-2 Crystal Palace, round 4 replay**
- ☻ **League Cup: Winners**
- ☻ **Europe: Champions League exit at first stage**
- ☻ **UEFA Cup: 1-3 (aggregate) Celtic, quarter-final**

Whereas Anfield was once a fortress, in 2002-03 the Big Bad Asthmatic Wolf could have blown Liverpool's house down. They won fewer than half their home games in the League while in Cup competitions they suffered embarrassing Anfield defeats to Crystal Palace and Celtic. There were even calls for Jimmy Corkhill to take over as manager. Yet Gérard Houllier's men had started solidly, staying unbeaten in their first dozen League games, but after a 1-0 defeat at Middlesbrough in November the rot set in. Still, as long as El Hadji Diouf was in the side, they remained within spitting distance of the leaders. The trouble was that Diouf and the other new summer signings, fellow Senegalese Salif Diao and French import Bruno Cheyrou, proved big disappointments. Their failure to deliver was worthy of the Royal Mail. Meanwhile the centre of defence was so slow it was declared a pedestrian zone, and in goal Jerzy Dudek's handling evoked comparisons with Heathrow baggage staff

THEIR FAILURE TO DELIVER WAS WORTHY OF THE ROYAL MAIL

One for the album: Emile Heskey shows strength and determination.

on the night flight to Malaga. So it was a good job Liverpool could rely on the goals of Emile Heskey – all six of them. This was the season when Virgin Atlantic named two new planes after the Liverpool strikers. One plane was named Michael Owen because it was fast and direct; the other was named Emile Heskey because it had a turning circle of ten minutes.

A team containing Steven Gerrard and Owen should have been major contenders but Houllier had, for the most part, surrounded his two genuine artists with a bunch of cowboy decorators. The upshot was that Liverpool were knocked out of the FA Cup early, Europe twice and finished nineteen points behind their friends from Old Trafford, fifth place meaning that they failed to qualify for the following season's Champions League. All they had to show for a season that had promised much was the worthless Worthington Cup. They couldn't even

⚽ ODDBALL

ROBBIE FOWLER WAS ONCE SIDELINED FROM THE LIVERPOOL TEAM WITH A KNEE INJURY AFTER HE STRETCHED TO PICK UP HIS TV REMOTE CONTROL.

complete their Panini stickers album: Dudek was missing. Nothing new there then.

Scotland
2002-04

Let's face it, the union of Scotland and Berti Vogts was the unlikeliest since John Major and Edwina Currie. The little chap had excellent credentials, having coached Germany to the Euro '96 title, but the general feeling was that the Scottish FA didn't need a foreign coach to make a mess of things – they were doing a perfectly good job of that themselves. If Berti's early results with Scotland scarcely suggested that he was the nation's Messiah, his growing army of critics had a field day when his new charges opened their Euro 2004 qualifiers against the Faeroe Islands, the footballing equivalent of the amoeba.

THE WORST SCOTTISH PERFORMANCE IN 130 YEARS

After thirteen minutes the Scots were two goals down, thanks to a level of organization not seen since the Keystone Cops. Although they fought back for a draw, the press labelled it the worst performance in 130 years of Scottish football. The *Scotsman* wrote witheringly: 'David Weir and Christian Dailly gave a demonstration of the art of the central defender of which Ally McCoist would have been ashamed.' Thereafter Berti's name rarely appeared in the Scottish press without the prefix 'bumbling'.

With Berti continuing to hand out

Scotland's Paul Dickov has the can-can down to a fine art but the football, as the Faeroe Islands discovered to their joy in this match in 2002, was a bit more slipshod.

international caps like sweeties, Scotland blundered their way through the group before crashing out 6-1 on aggregate to Holland in a play-off. The finals in Portugal would be for the grown-ups. In February 2004 Berti's men were on the receiving end of a 4-0 friendly drubbing by Wales, which is roughly on a par with a professional boxer being knocked out by Jarvis Cocker.

With Berti's reputation in tatters, a good start to the 2006 World Cup qualifiers was essential but his tactics remained harder to fathom than a Garth Crooks question. Instead Scotland picked up just two points from three games – scrambled draws against Slovenia and Moldova – at which point Berti quit after two-and-a-half years in charge. He said he had resigned because the supporters clearly wanted him out. It was one of the few things he got right. In some ways Berti Vogts would be a tough act to follow … but then so was Richard Nixon.

⚽ ODDBALL

FOLLOWING A VIOLENT MATCH WITH RANGERS IN 1988, HEARTS DIRECTOR DOUGLAS PARK LOCKED SCOTTISH REFEREE DAVID SYME IN HIS DRESSING ROOM AND HID THE KEY.

EVERTON
2003-04

- ☻ **League: 17th (Premiership)**
- ☻ **FA Cup: 1-2 Fulham, round 4**
- ☻ **League Cup: 4-5 (on penalties) Middlesbrough, round 4**

This was the season when Everton were supposed to become a force in the land once more. They had a bright young manager in David Moyes and in his first year in charge he had led them to a highly respectable finishing place of seventh. And they had the Boy Wonder, Wayne Rooney, the most exciting young talent in English football. Some fans were barely old enough for their first ASBO the last time there was this much optimism around Goodison Park.

THE SEASON PROVED A MASSIVE ANTI-CLIMAX

At times Rooney has played like Gary Lineker, Kevin Keegan and Michael Owen all rolled into one. But for him and girlfriend Colleen – the council-house Posh and Becks – the season proved a massive anti-climax. Rooney couldn't buy a goal (and Colleen must have tried), ending up with just nine to his name in the League. Even Rooney's grandmother could have put away some of the chances he missed. This would not be the last time the words 'Rooney' and 'grandmother' would be used in the same sentence. Without his input Everton never lived up to expectations. Goals were in short supply throughout and the team closed the season with just one win in ten games, culminating in a five-goal thumping at Manchester City. Their total of thirty-nine points was Everton's lowest for over a hundred years, but was just enough to enable them to cling to their Premiership status.

After defeat to lowly Wolves a furious Moyes raged at the players and cancelled their golf social. Almost overnight the new Alex Ferguson had become the new Ally MacLeod. There were dark mutterings that Moyes had lost the dressing room – something that Cloughie probably did at Forest in a tired and emotional moment. But what a difference a summer made. Rooney moved on to pastures new and a new mellow Moyes emerged, kinder to the skin. Everyone was happy. Moyes had a willing, energetic new team, Rooney had got his dream move and Colleen had enough money to keep her badly dressed for life.

⊗ ODDBALL

TWICE IN THE SPACE OF FOUR DAYS IN MARCH 1972 EVERTON DEFENDER TOMMY WRIGHT SCORED OWN-GOALS INSIDE THE FIRST MINUTE, FIRST AGAINST LIVERPOOL AND THEN AGAINST MANCHESTER UNITED.

Everton's Lee Carsley does sit-ups in punishment for being part of such a crap team while Rooney looks on and dreams of transfers.

LEEDS UNITED

2003-04

- ☻ **League: 19th (Premiership)**
- ☻ **FA Cup: 1-4 Arsenal, round 3**
- ☻ **League Cup: 2-3 Manchester United, round 3**

There are some hard jobs in football – refereeing a Milan derby; drawing up a five-year plan to get Halifax Town into the Premiership; acting as Craig Bellamy's public relations advisor; but managing Leeds United over the past few years must rank as one of the toughest. Leeds have paid the price for the extravagance of former chairman Peter Ridsdale, whose spending spree made Elton John look like Scrooge. Among his purchases were eleven tropical fish in the Leeds colours of blue, yellow and white. Presumably if he had been chairman of Newcastle he would have bought a herd of zebras to graze on the pitch. Arguably his greatest extravagance was hiring Terry Venables in July 2002. Venables wasted no time in splashing out £2.75m on old chum Nick Barmby (Terry Fenwick must have been on holiday). Predictably the love affair between Ridsdale and Venables soon ended in a messy break-up in March 2003 and Peter Reid was brought in to turn things round and stave off relegation. But Elland Road was like DFS – every day a sale. Rio Ferdinand, Jonathan Woodgate and

ELLAND ROAD WAS LIKE DFS – EVERY DAY A SALE

Harry Kewell had all been sold to balance the books, leaving Reid to start the 2003-04 season with a squad so thin it was positively anorexic.

Reid made two grave errors that alienated the fans. One was dispensing with the services of his assistant, Eddie Gray, who had been at Leeds so long he could remember when Norman Hunter bit rusks rather than legs. The other was signing Brazilian World Cup winning defender Roque Junior. Taken on a one-year loan from AC Milan, Roque Junior was brushed aside by opposing strikers like an irritating flake of dandruff. He barely appeared to have the physique and resolve to cope with a Friday evening trip around Sainsbury's, let alone deal with the best forwards in the Premiership. He played only five League games and the Leeds faithful were mightily relieved when he returned from international duty with an Achilles injury, as a result of which he was sent back to Italy in January 2004. By then Reid had been sacked, with Leeds bottom of the table following a 6-1 thrashing at Portsmouth.

In a comeback worthy of Lazarus, Gray was appointed caretaker manager. Although still able to call upon the services of Alan Smith and Mark Viduka, Gray could not keep Leeds up. It would be second-tier football at Elland Road, with the only bright spot being that Barmby was on the road to Hull.

⚽ ODDBALL

FORMER LEEDS FULLBACK WILLIE BELL RESIGNED FROM HIS JOB AS LINCOLN CITY MANAGER IN 1978 TO JOIN A RELIGIOUS SECT IN AMERICA.

Mark Viduka on the way down and, in this case, out of the FA Cup against Arsenal.

Northern Ireland
2004 EUROPEAN CHAMPIONSHIPS QUALIFIERS

Northern Ireland have always been the caramel cup in the great chocolate box of European football – colourless, unfancied and really there only to make up the numbers. Apart from reaching the World Cup finals in 1958 and 1982 (optimism rears its ugly head once every quarter-century), Northern Ireland's history has been a catalogue of unremitting failure. Their lack of success has been comparable to that of Albania in the Eurovision Song Contest. But even by Northern Ireland standards their qualifying group for Euro 2004 was particularly dire. It would be the nation's Waterloo – although the quality was more Boom-Bang-a-Bang.

Between February 2002, when Steve Lomas scored against Poland, and February 2004, when David Healy was on the mark in a 4-1 defeat to Norway, Northern Ireland went a record 1,298 minutes without a goal. A one-eyed fisherman would have been more adept at finding the net. During that drought they failed to breach such flimsy defences as Liechtenstein, Cyprus and Armenia and plunged to 124th in the

A CATALOGUE OF UNREMITTING FAILURE

⚽ ODDBALL

MAKING HIS LEAGUE DEBUT FOR BARNET IN 1995, NORTHERN IRELAND KEEPER MAIK TAYLOR WAS BEATEN BY AN 80-YARD DROP KICK FROM HIS OPPOSITE NUMBER, HEREFORD UNITED'S CHRIS MACKENZIE.

FIFA world rankings – just below St Winifred's Girls' School Choir. Under manager Sammy McIlroy their eight qualifying group matches had one common factor – the word 'nil'. There seemed a better chance of Ian Paisley and Gerry Adams going out clubbing together than Northern Ireland ever scoring another goal.

After defeat to Greece in the final qualifier in October 2003 extended Northern Ireland's scoreless run to thirteen games McIlroy quit to become manager of Stockport County, who were then lurking dangerously close to the bottom of Division Two. Evidence that the strain had got to him came when he declared: 'Stockport have great ambition and potential.' Here was a man in need of a rest.

His successor, Lawrie Sanchez, broke the hoodoo in his first game in charge, thanks to Healy's goal, and, when Estonia were beaten 1-0 in a friendly at the end of March 2004, it was Northern Ireland's first win for nearly two-and-a-half years. They may not have reached orange cream status but at least they had made it up to hazelnut whirl.

Northern Ireland play so poorly even their manager can't bear to watch. Beleaguered Sammy McIlroy hangs his head in shame as Armenia thrash his boys.

SOUTHAMPTON
2004-05

⚽ **League: 20th (Premiership)**
⚽ **FA Cup: 0-4 Manchester United, round 6**
⚽ **League Cup: 2-5 Watford, round 4**

It didn't need Mystic Meg to predict troubled times ahead for Southampton when they sacked manager Paul Sturrock two games into the new season. One of the reasons cited for his abrupt exit was his poor dress sense, which apparently upset certain members of the board. While Sturrock may not have been catwalk material, there isn't exactly a rush to recruit Martin Jol as the next James Bond or to put Arsène Wenger on *Celebrity Love Island*. Saints' ex-public schoolboy chairman Rupert Lowe replaced Sturrock with Steve Wigley who, although lacking any previous managerial experience, at least gave the impression that his wardrobe contained a suit. But by December a string of desperate results – including a League Cup trouncing at Watford – led Rupert to appoint tie-wearing Harry Redknapp as the club's twelfth manager in ten years.

REDKNAPP AND ASSISTANT JIM SMITH WERE NO MIRACLE WORKERS

To call Redknapp's appointment 'controversial' would be like describing Rik Waller as 'a bit chubby', for two weeks earlier Redknapp had resigned from Portsmouth and publicly stated that he would not be joining their bitter rivals. Pompey fans were baying for blood.

Their mood lightened somewhat when it became apparent that Redknapp and assistant Jim Smith (the Muttley to his Dick Dastardly) were no miracle workers. Southampton continued to hover in or around the relegation zone, their cause not helped when midfielder David Prutton picked up a ten-match ban for manhandling referee Alan Wiley. Quite what Mr Wiley had done to provoke such an uncharacteristic tantrum remains open to speculation – but rumour has it that he had threatened to ruffle Prutton's immaculately coiffed hair. And under Rupert's regime a hair out of place or a split end was punished by a fine of a week's wages. Dandruff brought about immediate termination of contract.

A four-goal drubbing at Portsmouth – where goalkeeper Antti Niemi played more like Harry's Auntie Naomi – hastened the decline and, when Southampton lost at home to Manchester United on the last day,

⚽ ODDBALL

WHEN HE WAS SOUTHAMPTON MANAGER GRAEME SOUNESS RECEIVED A CALL HE THOUGHT WAS FROM WORLD FOOTBALLER OF THE YEAR GEORGE WEAH, RECOMMENDING THIRTY-ONE-YEAR-OLD SENEGAL STRIKER ALI DIA. SOUNESS GAVE THE UNKNOWN A FIRST-TEAM GAME BUT SOON REALIZED HE HAD BEEN CONNED. THE CALL WAS A HOAX. AFTER A PREMIERSHIP CAREER LASTING JUST FIFTY-THREE MINUTES, ALI DIA WAS SHIPPED OFF TO SOMEWHERE NEARER HIS TRUE STANDARD – GATESHEAD.

they slid out of the top flight for the first time in twenty-seven years.

Still, as Rupert pointed out in his programme notes for that game, all was not doom and gloom. The club's radio station, catering facilities and shop were all flourishing, the latter presumably doing a nice line in red and white gents' blazers. Such progress will undoubtedly be appreciated by the team's new manager, Laurence Llewelyn-Bowen.

Southampton manager Harry Redknapp: no miracle worker.

SOILED SHORTS

⚽ When the Namibian women's football team lost an Olympic qualifying game 13-0 to South Africa in 2003, the defeat was blamed on the girls' lust for pornography. The team's hotel bill showed that they had watched six porn films on the eve of the match before finally going to bed in the early hours of the morning.

⚽ Play was held up in the match between Scunthorpe and Rochdale in April 2004 after Rochdale keeper Neil Edwards was nipped on the arm while trying to clear a goose off the pitch.

⚽ When a match between Sheffield team Stocksbridge Steels and Witton Albion was abandoned because of thick fog in 2003, all the players trooped back to the dressing room … except for Stocksbridge goalkeeper Richard Siddall who was unaware that the game had been called off. Unable to see beyond his penalty box, he merely assumed all the action was at the other end and stayed out on the pitch for another ten minutes before his teammates realized he was missing.

⚽ Incensed by jeering fans after a disappointing 1-1 draw with the Cape Verde Islands in a 2003 World Cup qualifier, Swaziland players suddenly ordered the driver to stop the team bus. They then jumped from the vehicle and, armed with sticks, chased their tormentors down the road.

⚽ Voted Leicester City's 1995–96 Player of the Year for his safe hands, goalkeeper Kevin Poole was presented with a cut-glass rose bowl … which he promptly dropped.

⚽ After Algeria had been knocked out of the qualifying rounds for the 1998 World Cup, the country's king was so angry that he banned the coach and his deputy from football for life and disbanded the National League.

⚽ On 2 April 1994 Scottish club Cowdenbeath beat Arbroath 1-0 to end a two-year run of thirty-eight home League games without a win.

⚽ While filming an advert in 2004 Brazilian soccer star Ronaldinho fluffed an overhead kick and ended up smashing a window at a twelfth-century Madrid cathedral.

⚽ Having lost all fourteen games at the start of the 1993–94 season, Thetford Town players were hypnotized in an attempt to improve their fortunes. They lost their next game 9-0.

⚽ After scoring from the penalty spot in 2004 Bayer Leverkusen goalkeeper Joerg Butt took so long to return to his goal following his celebrations that Schalke striker Mike Hanker scored from the centre circle direct from the restart.

⚽ During a game between Belgian teams Young Stars Eeklo and FC Zelzate in 2004 a fan ran on to the pitch and pulled down the shorts and pants of referee Jacky Temmerman.

⚽ A Somerset footballer hit a crucial penalty over the bar after a female opposition supporter flashed her breasts at him from behind the goal. With the game finishing 0-0 after extra time, the 2003 Morland Challenge Cup Final between Norton Hill Rangers and Wookey FC went to penalties. Cruelly distracted by a woman lifting her shirt as he ran up to the ball, a Rangers player ballooned his spot kick into the car park, allowing Wookey to triumph 3-2. A spot of 'Wookey nookie' had won the day …

☻ Norwegian referee Per Arne Brataas confessed in 2003 that he tried to avoid handing out red and yellow cards because he suffers from dyslexia and can't face writing post-match reports.

☻ The Wheatsheaf pub team from St Helen's Auckland, County Durham, achieved the distinction of finishing the 1994-95 season with fewer points than they started with. They drew one and lost the other twenty-nine League games but were also docked two points for failing to field a team on one occasion. So they ended up with a points total of minus one.

☻ Montserrat were officially named the worst national team in the world in 2002. In the play-off for last place Montserrat, 203rd in the FIFA rankings, were beaten 4-0 by the Himalayan kingdom of Bhutan, ranked one position higher. A crowd of 25,000 masochists turned up to witness the clash of the clueless.

PICTURE ACKNOWLEDGEMENTS

p. 2   Barratts / EMPICS / Alpha

p. 6   Peter Robinson / EMPICS

p. 8-9   S&G / EMPICS / Alpha

p. 13   Getty Images

p. 16   Getty Images

p. 18-9   S & G / Alpha / EMPICS

p. 22   Getty Images

p. 24-5   © popperfoto.com

p. 27   © popperfoto.com

p. 30   SMG / EMPICS

p. 34-5   Getty Images

p. 37   Bildbyran / EMPICS / Bildbyran

p. 40-1   Getty Images

p. 43   Alan Cozzie / Offside

p. 47   Mark Leech / Offside

p. 50   Malcolm Gilson / Rex Features

p. 52   Getty Images

p. 56   Mark Leech / Offside

p. 59   Mark Leech / Offside

p. 62   Getty Images

p. 65   Neal Simpson / EMPICS

p. 68   Mark Leech / Offside

p. 71   PA / EMPICS

p. 74   EMPICS

p. 77   © popperfoto.com

p. 80   Phil O'Brien / EMPICS

p. 83   Ross Kinnaird / EMPICS

p. 86   Matthew Ashton / EMPICS

p. 88   Ross Kinnaird / EMPICS

p. 92-3   Ross Kinnaird / EMPICS

p. 95   Steve Morton / EMPICS

p. 99   Laurence Griffiths / EMPICS

p. 101   Steve Morton / EMPICS

p. 104-5   Dave Kendall / PA / EMPICS

p. 107   Neal Simpson / EMPICS

p. 109   Barry Coombs / EMPICS

p. 112   David Cheskin / PA / EMPICS

p. 115   Tony Marshall / EMPICS

p. 119   Getty Images

p. 122   Matthew Ashton / EMPICS

p. 125   ABACA / EMPICS

p. 128   Matthew Ashton / EMPICS

p. 130   Mike Egerton / EMPICS

p. 133   David Davies / PA / EMPICS

p. 137   Tony Marshall / EMPICS

p. 140   John Walton / EMPICS

p. 143   Michael Cooper / EMPICS

p. 146   Getty Images